THE CHEMISTRY OF THE BLOOD

THE CHEMISTRY OF THE BLOOD

M. R. DeHaan, M.D.

ZondervanPublishingHouse
Grand Rapids, Michigan

A Division of HarperCollinsPublishers

THE CHEMISTRY OF THE BLOOD

Copyright © 1943 by Zondervan Publishing House
Copyright renewed 1981 by Ruth Haaksma

Requests for information should be addressed to:
Zondervan Publishing House
Grand Rapids, Michigan 49530

ISBN 0-310-23291-0

Printed in the United States of America

CONTENTS

Foreword

Contents

FOREWORD

Regarding the publication of the following messages on the scientific aspects of the Gospel of the Grace of God, an explanatory statement is in order.

All of these sermons were first preached over the coast-to-coast network of the Mutual Broadcasting System and have been chosen from the many others delivered over the same network, first, with reference to the popular need as seen in the mail response, and second, with reference to the evident blessing of God upon these messages as reflected in the reports of definite conversions of radio listeners.

The following messages were first published in the form of small booklets, but by popular demand these carefully selected sermons have been bound in one volume under the title of *The Chemistry of the Blood*. If these messages in a single volume are blessed of God as the individual messages were, I shall be more than repaid for the effort entailed in giving this book to the public.

We send these messages out with the believing prayer that God will bless His Word in the establishment of saints, the salvation of sinners, the exaltation of His own Word, and for His glory alone.

As a physician and surgeon for many years, and now as a physician of souls, I have sought to make known the divine remedy for man's awful illness of sin. May the Great Physician Himself apply the Word by His precious Holy Spirit.

M. R. DeHaan, M.D.

Grand Rapids, Michigan

THE
CHEMISTRY
OF THE
BLOOD

CHAPTER 1

THE CHEMISTRY OF THE BLOOD

I

> Moreover ye shall eat no manner of blood, whether it be of fowl or of beast, in any of your dwellings. Whatsoever soul it be that eateth any manner of blood, even that soul shall be cut off from his people (Leviticus 7:26, 27).

The Bible is a Book of blood and a bloody Book. When we are accused of preaching a Gospel of blood we proudly plead guilty to the charge, for the only thing that gives life to our teaching and power to the Word of God is the fact that it is the blood which is the very life and power of the Gospel. The Bible declares itself to be a "living" Book, the only living Book in the world; and it is able to impart life to those who will believe with their hearts what it teaches. In Hebrews 4 we read these words:

> The word of God is quick, and powerful, and sharper than any twoedged sword.

The word translated "quick" in this verse is "LIVING" or "ALIVE." The Word of God is a living Word, wholly distinct from all other books for just one reason, namely, that it contains blood circulating through every page and in every verse. From Genesis to Revelation we see the stream of blood which imparts to this Book the very life of God. Without the blood the Bible would be like any other book and of no more value, for the Bible plainly teaches that the life is in the blood. As we begin this message on the blood, therefore, we must begin with one fundamental principle found in the Bible. This fundamental principle is given in Leviticus 17 and reads as follows:

> For the life of the flesh is in the blood: and I have given it
> to you upon the altar to make an atonement for your souls:
> for it is the blood that maketh an atonement for the soul
> (Leviticus 17:11).

This same inspired principle is repeated in the fourteenth
verse where we read again:

> For it [the blood] is the life of all flesh; the blood of it is
> for the life thereof.

Life, that mysterious something which scientists have never yet
been able to define or fathom, is said by God to be in the
blood of the flesh, so that there can be no life without the blood.
Although this is true of all flesh, we are mainly interested in
the human blood and particularly in the blood of the Man
Christ Jesus because in His blood was not only life as we think
of it physically, but ETERNAL life as well.

THE PHYSIOLOGY OF BLOOD

In the human body there are many different kinds of tissues.
We define them as muscle, nerve, fat, gland, bone, connective
tissues, etc. All these tissues have one thing in common: they
are fixed cells, microscopically small and having a specific and
limited function. Unlike these fixed tissues, the blood is fluid
and mobile, that is, it is not limited to one part of the body
but is free to move throughout the entire body and supply the
fixed cells with nourishment and carry off the waste products
and the "ashes" of cell activity, a process which we call metabolism. In the normal human body there are about five quarts
of this fluid, and this blood pumped by the heart circulates
through the system about every twenty-three seconds, so that
every cell in the body is constantly supplied and cleansed and
at the same time is in constant communication with every other
cell in that body. This blood is the most mysterious of all tissues,
being composed of scores of elements and compounds and
strange chemical bodies, whose function is not yet fully understood, but all of which have to do with the mystery of life,
for the *life...is in the blood*. Once the blood fails to reach
the cells and members of the body, they promptly die and no

man ever dies until his blood ceases to circulate. This life is in the blood.

THE BLOOD OF CHRIST

Now all this is true of a physical body, but all points to a greater, deeper spiritual truth. The Church of Jesus Christ is called His body and *we are members of his body* and *severally members one of another*. In this body Jesus Christ is the Head and all believers are the members. These members are related by the blood of Christ. The life of each member depends on His blood and is dependent solely for life, nourishment, cleansing and growth upon the blood of the Lamb of God, for *the life . . . is in the blood*. Every born-again believer is a member of that body and lives the common life of every other member by the one thing which unites them and makes them "relatives and brothers," even the blood of Christ. These members may be widely separated in the body; they may differ widely in color; they may differ widely in function, or differ in structure, but they are all members of one body and united by the one tissue, the blood that reaches every member everywhere. Even so it is with the body of Christ, the true Church. Its members may differ in color, and be white or black or yellow. They may differ in their location as far as Eskimos are removed from the Boers in South Africa. They may differ in form as much as Catholics and Plymouth Brethren, but all born-again believers who have trusted the finished work of the Lord Jesus Christ, the Head of the body, are brothers by blood, members of one family and body, whether they be Jews or Gentiles, white or black, Catholic or Protestant, kings or peasants. All are one through the blood of the Lord Jesus Christ.

ALL ONE BY THE BLOOD

Listen, my friend, God cares nothing about our man-made divisions and groups and is not interested in our self-righteous, hairsplitting and religious, man-made formulas and organizations. He wants you to recognize the UNITY of the body of Christ. Our business is not building denominations and proselyting men and women from one faith to another but to preach the truth that *Ye must be born again* and that you are lost no matter what church you belong to unless you have been washed in the precious blood of Christ. Show me the man or the woman who is more interested in getting members for his church than winning them for Christ, and I will show you a person who does not yet know the unifying and purifying power of the blood, in making us all ONE in Him, not in form or ritual or mode of worship, but one in common interest to EXALT OUR HEAD, the Lord Jesus, and to love one another. Some folk are so busy defending their pet doctrines and sectarian views and getting church members, that they never win a soul for Christ.

ALL RELATED BY BLOOD

All men are related by the blood of Adam, sinful and polluted blood, dead in trespasses and in sins. Scripture teaches that God —

> hath made of one blood all nations of men for to dwell on all the face of the earth (Acts 17:26).

All men have a "common" origin in Adam. All men are blood relatives of Adam, whether they be white or black, Jew or Gentile, pagan or cultured. Their blood carries the sentence of death because of Adam's sin, and for this reason all men die a common death, with no exceptions. Remember that the life is in the blood, and so if man must die it is because there is death in the blood. Although we do not know the nature of the fruit of the tree of knowledge of good and evil, we do know that the eating of it caused "blood poisoning" and resulted in death, for God had said:

> The day that thou eatest thereof thou shalt surely die.

So potent was this poison that six thousand years after, all who are related to Adam by human birth still succumb to that poison of sin which is carried in some way in the blood. A review of the story of Adam's creation will make clear this truth. We are told that God formed man out of the dust of the earth. Up to this time Adam was a lifeless clump of clay. Materially he was just so much dust, and merely molded into the shape of a man, but without life; he was a mere dummy. Then the record tells us that —

> God . . . breathed into his nostrils the breath of life; and man became a living soul.

The breath of God put something in man that made him ALIVE. That something was blood. It must have been. It could be nothing else: for we have already shown that the *life of the flesh is in the blood* and so when life was added by the breath of God, He imparted blood to that lump of clay in the shape of a man, and man became a living soul. Adam's body was of the ground. His blood was the separate gift of God, for God is Life and the Author of all life.

SIN AND DEATH

Then man sinned and ate of the tree of the knowledge of good and evil and HE DIED — DIED SPIRITUALLY and, ultimately, physically. Since life is in the blood, when man died, something happened to the blood. Sin affected the blood of man, not his body, except indirectly, because it is supplied by the blood. For this very reason flesh can only be called *sinful* flesh because it is nourished and fed and sustained by sinful blood. And since God *hath made of one blood all nations,* sin is present in all of Adam's progeny. For in that one sinned all have sinned.

THE VIRGIN BIRTH

This very fact that sin affected the blood of man necessitated the VIRGIN BIRTH of Christ if He was to be a son of Adam and yet a sinless man. For this very reason Christ could partake of Adam's flesh, which is not inherently sinful, but He could not partake of Adam's blood, which was completely sinful. God provided a way by which Jesus, *born of a woman* (not man), could be a perfect human being, but, because He had not a drop of Adam's blood in His veins, He did not share in Adam's sin. We discuss the subject of the virgin birth more fully elsewhere in this book, but we mention this thought here to further prove the statement that human blood is sinful and the whole plan of redemption, therefore, revolves around the blood.

II

> For if the blood of bulls and of goats, and the ashes of an heifer sprinkling the unclean, sanctifieth to the purifying of the flesh:
>
> How much more shall the blood of Christ, who through the eternal Spirit offered himself without spot to God, purge your conscience from dead works to serve the living God? (Hebrews 9:13-14).

The whole plan of redemption rests upon the power of the blood of the Lord Jesus Christ. We have pointed out that the blood is the only tissue which is unlimited in its movement within the body. Almost all other body tissues are fixed, such as muscle, bone, nerve, fat and skin. They remain where they are. The blood is the only tissue which is not fixed but circulates throughout the body to every living cell. There are other fluid products of the body, such as saliva and gastric juices, tears and bile, but these are not tissues, but secretions, and are not parts of the body but products of that body. The blood alone is the liquid tissue that can reach every single cell in the body and, therefore, unites all the members with the head and the individual members as well.

MYSTERIOUS STRUCTURE

Man has learned a great deal about this blood since the discovery of the microscope and the development of blood chemistry, and although much is still a mystery, we have a reasonably thorough understanding of its physical structure. The normal human body with its five quarts of blood is wholly dependent upon the circulation of this fluid for its life, for the *life of the flesh is in the blood.* Simply stated, the blood consists of a liquid vehicle called the *plasma,* a colorless liquid in which are suspended the various cellular elements and in which are found in solution a great many chemical compounds. The solid part of the blood consists mainly of three kinds of cells. These are called *platelets,* thin transparent cells whose function is still quite obscure. Then there are the red cells or *erythrocytes,* in the concentration of about 5,000,000 per cubic millimeter. These are the cells which carry the fuel to the tissues in the form of combined oxygen and which give the blood its red color. There are also the white cells or *leucocytes,* of which there are several kinds, which have to do particularly with the defense of the body in combatting infection. Other elements in solution provide for the clotting of the blood when an artery or vein is severed, and the *antibodies* prevent disease.

THE ERYTHROCYTES

A good deal is known concerning the red and the white cells, since they are the more easily studied. The red cells or *erythrocytes* are minute disc-shaped cells containing a mysterious substance called *hemoglobin,* an iron compound which has an affinity for oxygen, a fuel of the body. These red cells traveling through the lungs come in contact with the oxygen in the air we breathe and unite loosely with it to form oxy-hemoglobin; in that form they travel to all the cells and there discharge their little cargo to the cell, thus providing it with its vital oxygen for combustion and heat. Then the blood picks up the waste products of the tissues, the carbon dioxide, and the wastes of tissue metabolism, which we may well call "the cell garbage," and discharges this through the kidneys, the skin, the bowels and the lungs and then refills with a load of precious oxygen and repeats the entire cycle again, taking about twenty-three seconds for one trip around. The food is carried to the tissues by the blood and in the same vehicle the "garbage" is carried off, and yet there is never any contamination, so perfectly has the great Creator made us. Imagine our city produce dealers today delivering our foods unpackaged in the same truck in which they haul the garbage! Here is something at which our health departments may well wonder.

CHRIST OUR SUPPLY

As essential then as the blood is to our bodies, so essential is the blood of the Lord Jesus Christ to the body of Christ. It, too, is fluid, so that it can reach every single member of that body no matter how far those members may be removed the one from the other. Just as the blood supplies the food elements for nourishment and life, and then carries off the waste products and poisons due to cell metabolism, so, too, the Lord Jesus Christ is to every believer the only Source of life, the only support and sustenance of life, but also the One who keeps cleansing us day by day, so that our eternal life is really ETERNAL, for the *blood of Jesus Christ his Son cleanseth us from all sin.*

> Have you been to Jesus for the cleansing pow'r?
> Are YOU washed in the blood of the Lamb?
> Are your garments spotless? Are they white as snow?
> Are you washed in the blood of the Lamb?

Here indeed is a marvel of divine chemistry! In Revelation we read that the saints of God had washed their robes white in the blood of the Lamb. Think of it — washing in blood and becoming white! Wash your robes in the blood of a man and see what color they are. It is impossible to wash clothes white in human blood, but God's chemical laboratory of redemption has provided a way to wash away all filth and stain, and wonder of wonders, it is by washing in the BLOOD of the Lamb. His sinless, supernatural blood alone can do that.

THE LEUCOCYTES

In addition to the red cells in the blood plasma, we mentioned the white cells, scientifically called *leucocytes*. They are called "white cells" because they are pale or white in appearance, whereas the red cells, of course, are not. These white cells are somewhat larger than the red cells but fewer in number. They normally occur in the concentration of about four thousand to seven thousand per cubic millimeter, whereas the red cells have had a count of from four to five million. However, the number of these white cells may be very, very rapidly increased in cases of emergency. The seven thousand normal count may be called the regular "standing army" of the blood stream. When an infection occurs anywhere in the body and the body is attacked by an enemy "army" of germs, the news is flashed back to the "camp" where the white cells are manufactured and immediately the organ turns out a greatly increased number of these white cells and rushes them to the point of infection.

We might well call this "conscription of the white army" in time of emergency. The number of white cells is doubled and then trebled, for the white cells are the "soldiers" of the body. They have the strange power to kill germs and engulf them. So when you prick your finger and infection starts, you soon notice a swelling around the wound. This is caused by blood being rushed to the area carrying these little "soldiers," the white cells. These white cells surround the point of infection completely and lay siege to the bacteria causing the trouble. Millions of "soldiers" are killed and are gathered in one place, where they form what is commonly known as "pus."

So now the battle is turning and the wound which at first was red and angry and swollen now comes to a head. It has been successfully surrounded and finally the pimple bursts and the pus is expelled. The pus consists of serum and dead "soldiers," millions of the white cells which gave their lives in the battle for the body, together with countless numbers of germs partly digested by the white cells.

When the "dead" in the form of pus have been expelled, the blood and other white cells come in, clean up the "battlefield" and build new tissues, until all is healed and nothing but a scar remains. The number of white cell "soldiers" during all this time had been greatly increased, but now the battle is over and they return to their normal peace-time number. This is the reason the doctor takes a little of your blood out of your finger for a blood count when he suspects infection anywhere. In doubtful cases of appenciditis he takes a drop of blood and examines it. If the white cells are greatly increased and the "army" is being "conscripted" as indicated by the increasing number of little white "soldiers," he can be fairly certain that there is an attack by infection being made upon the body. Surely in the light of all this we can appreciate the words of David when he said, *I am fearfully and wonderfully made.*

OVERCOMING BY THE BLOOD

What the blood in our bodies does for us in times of danger and attack the PRECIOUS BLOOD of the Lord Jesus Christ does for each and every believer. In this connection I must quote a passage from Revelation 12:

> And I heard a loud voice saying in heaven, Now is come salvation, and strength, and the kingdom of our God, and the power of his Christ: for the accuser of our brethren is cast down, WHICH ACCUSED THEM BEFORE OUR GOD DAY AND NIGHT. AND THEY OVERCAME HIM BY THE BLOOD OF THE LAMB and by the word of their testimony (Revelation 12:10-11).

They overcame Him (Satan) BY THE BLOOD OF THE LAMB. Now this refers to the nation of Israel in the Tribulation, but it applies just as well to us today. Satan is the accuser of the brethren. He brings charges against us before God, and, to be sure, there are plenty of charges to be made. But when He comes before God to accuse us, there is One there, even our great HIGH PRIEST, the Lamb of God, and all He needs to do is to point to the blood that was shed for us and it is enough.

Sometimes Satan also comes to accuse us. He points out our sins and failures and we see our shortcomings and the sins of the flesh and he says, "Are you a Christian? Are you saved? You don't look like a Christian." The result is that often we go down and are defeated when we look at ourselves and our sins. We begin to doubt our salvation and question our redemption. How can we overcome this enemy? How shall we meet this infection? There is only one answer: *They overcame him by the blood of the Lamb.*

I see no good in myself — even less than the Devil sees. I have no hope in myself and have no confidence in the flesh. Then I plead the blood. I look to Calvary and point to Him who there died for me and shed His blood for me, and the light breaks through. I see that it is not my goodness nor the awful mountain of my sins, but it all depends on His blood. The blood fights for me. It is the army of "white cells" in the blood of Christ which puts the enemy to flight. I acknowledge my sin, I do not deny it and then I claim the promise:

> If we confess our sins, he is faithful and just to forgive us our sins, and to CLEANSE US FROM ALL UNRIGHTEOUSNESS (I John 1:9).
>
> If we walk in the light, as he is in the light, we have fellowship one with another, and the blood of Jesus Christ his Son cleanseth us from all sin (I John 1:7).
>
> They overcame him by the blood of the Lamb (Rev. 12:11).

IMMUNITY TO SIN

We have time for just a word about a few other elements in the blood. In the blood are not only these cells and the clotting elements but science has discovered in the blood the ANTIBODIES or ANTITOXINS. These are elements which PREVENT INFECTION. The white cells fight infection when it occurs, but the ANTIBODIES prevent the infection from getting a foothold. Their nature is not fully understood, but we know clearly that except for these disease-preventing elements we would soon perish. It is of interest to note that these antibodies are produced in response to infection. That is, while these bodies which prevent a certain disease may be absent in the blood, AFTER THE PERSON HAS ONCE HAD THE DISEASE, these bodies have been produced in a large amount, and thus prevent him from contracting the same disease twice. Some of these antibodies last for life, as in the case of smallpox, scarlet fever and other diseases. Once you have had such a disease, you will never contract it again. Other antibodies are only temporarily effective, giving immunity only for a time, so that after a certain period of time the same disease may be contracted again. The thing to notice is this: The body once attacked by disease builds up immunity so that it will not be attacked by that disease again. This immunity is in the blood.

THE BLOOD OF CHRIST

A great lesson unfolds before us when we apply these facts to the blood of Christ. Even after we have been saved we are still open to the attacks of the world, the flesh and the Devil. Even after being born again we all too often fall prey to temptation and go down. The characteristic of the Christian who fails is that he seeks the cleansing of the blood of Christ and thereafter pleads the blood of Christ and guards against a repetition of the thing that once brought him down. He does not fall into the same sin again and again, for each experience builds up an immunity against that sin.

The difference between the sinner and the saint is that the saint HATES his sin and pleads the blood of Christ, whereas the sinner loves his sin and goes back into it. The saint is like a sheep. It may fall in the mud hole, but it is not comfortable there, and will bleat until the shepherd lifts it out, and thereafter will avoid that mud hole by ten rods. The sinner is like a pig. It goes about looking for slime pits and when it finds one it slides in with a grunt of glee and will squeal vehement objections if you try to pull it out, and no sooner is it out than it will return to the slime pit again.

The saint may FALL into sin but he will never remain there, and he will be unhappy while in it. Oh, Christian, do not despair if you have failed. Our precious Lord knew when He came to die for you what a failure you would be. He knew how hard it would be to remain undefiled in this old world which is "no friend to grace." He knew the pitfalls in the way and the deceitfulness of the flesh, and so when He died to save you, He also shed His blood to cleanse you, for He caused John to write:

> If we say that we have no sin, we deceive ourselves, and the truth is not in us.
> IF WE CONFESS OUR SINS, he is faithful and just to forgive us our sins, and to cleanse us from all unrighteousness (I John 1:8-9).

My friend, it will do you no good to deny your sins. God says if you do that you are only deceiving YOURSELF and nobody else. Your only hope is in CONFESSION of your sin, and then He sends the "army" of "white cells" of the precious blood of Christ to cleanse you. Then TRUST Him to keep you from sin through that same precious blood which, in addition to the "white cells" of fighting and cleansing, also contains the ANTI-TOXIN against further sinning. Do not despair today as you think of how you have failed, but flee to Him who shed HIS

PRECIOUS BLOOD for your salvation, your cleansing and your KEEPING.

III

> God that made the world and all things therein, seeing that he is Lord of heaven and earth, dwelleth not in temples made with hands;
> Neither is worshipped with men's hands, as though he needed any thing, seeing he giveth to all life, and breath, and all things:
> And hath made of one blood all nations of men for to dwell on all the face of the earth (Acts 17:24-26).

One statement in this passage calls for special attention. Paul says that God *hath made of one blood all nations of men for to dwell on all the face of the earth.* The one thing which relates all men to each other is the blood that flows in their veins. ALL MEN ARE OF ONE BLOOD and that ONE BLOOD was the blood of Father Adam, the first man and the progenitor of the whole human race.

Since the LIFE is in the blood, according to the Scriptures, and the wages of sin is death, sin affected the blood of Adam and caused him to die. Because the blood of all men partakes of the sin of Adam, it can only be cleansed by the application of sinless blood, *for it is the blood that maketh an atonement for the soul.* As the first Adam's sin corrupted the blood of the entire human family, so the pure sinless blood of the last Adam makes atonement for the sin of the world. *For without shedding of blood is no remission ... It is the blood that maketh an atonement for the soul.* Eve's sin does not affect us, although Eve sinned before Adam did. It was the SIN OF ADAM which brought death upon the whole race because it is ADAM'S SEED. ONLY Jesus is called the Seed of the woman, because He was born of a woman and thus His blood was without the sin of Adam. Jesus could have a human body, but He was not a sinner like you and me because He was born of woman by the Holy Spirit. There was then only one remedy for SIN: sinless blood; and only one could supply this, even the sinless Son of God.

From Genesis to Revelation we have this message of the

atoning blood. In the Old Testament, we have it in the example of the blood of the lambs and the goats which were slain in the bloody ritual of Israel. Long, long before the perfect Lamb of God Himself came, the Lord was preparing the world for Him by the multitudinous types in the Old Testament. Without blood there could be no atonement, and until the blood was presented the holy law of God demanded justice and death for the sinner. That is why, when God gave the two tables of the law to Moses upon Mount Sinai — the law which called for justice and not mercy, the law which said, *The soul that sinneth it shall die,* the law which demanded PERFECTION or death — He also gave to Moses on the same Mount the pattern of the Tabernacle, which was indeed built on blood and whose whole ritual was bathed in blood. God knew when He gave the law to Israel that they could not keep it perfectly and MUST DIE, and so in mercy He gave the Tabernacle and the altar and the blood so that a sinning people condemned by the law might have life through the sheltering blood.

GOD'S PERFECT LAMB

The blood of bulls and goats and lambs could not atone for sin, but merely pointed forward to the One that would come in the end of that age to PUT AWAY SIN by the sacrifice of Himself. So in the fullness of time God sent forth His Son into the world to be born of a woman, and at the end of His life He shed His precious eternal blood ONCE and for all. After that there was no more sacrifice. The blood of the sacrificial animals of the Old Testament was corruptible and decayed and was soon gone, but the blood shed on Calvary was imperishable blood. It is called *incorruptible.* Peter says:

> Forasmuch as ye know that ye were not redeemed with corruptible things, as silver and gold . . . but with the precious blood of Christ. . . .

The blood of the Lord Jesus is sinless blood, and since it is sinless, it is incorruptible, for sin brings corruption, and where no sin is there is no corruption. Elsewhere in this book we shall point out why the blood which flowed in Jesus' body was sinless. Every drop of blood which flowed in Jesus' body is still in existence, and is just as fresh as it was when it flowed from His wounded brow and hands and feet and side. The blood that flowed from His unbroken skin in Gethsemane, the blood that was smeared about His back when the cruel, weighted thongs cut through His flesh as the flagellator scourged Him, the blood that oozed out under the thorny crown and flowed from His hands, His head, His feet was never destroyed for it was incorruptible blood. David in speaking of Him in the sixteenth Psalm, which Peter quotes in Acts 2, says:

> Thou wilt not leave my soul in hell; neither wilt thou suffer thine Holy One to see corruption.

Although the body of the Lord Jesus Christ lay in the tomb in death for three days and three nights, no corruption entered it for that body contained incorruptible blood. Lazarus being dead only one day more was said by his sister to be STINKING with corruption, but this One saw no corruption because the only cause of corruption, SINFUL BLOOD, was absent from His flesh. That blood, every drop of it, is still in existence. Perhaps when the great High Priest ascended into heaven. He went, like the high priest of old, into the Holy of Holies, in the presence of God, to sprinkle the blood upon the Mercy Seat in heaven, of which the material Mercy Seat and Ark in the Tabernacle were merely copies. In Hebrews we read:

> It was therefore necessary that the patterns of things in the heavens [referring to the earthly Tabernacle] should be purified with these [that is, the blood of beasts]; but the heavenly things themselves with BETTER SACRIFICES THAN THESE.
> For Christ is not entered into the holy places made with hand, which are the figures of the true; but into heaven itself, now to appear in the presence of God for us:
> Nor yet that he should offer himself often, as the high priest entereth into the holy place every year with blood of others ... but now once in the end of the whole world hath he appeared to PUT AWAY SIN by the sacrifice of himself (Hebrews 9:23-26).

After Christ had made the atonement, He arose from the tomb, and then, as the eternal High Priest, ascended into heaven to present the blood in the Holy of Holies where God dwells, and that blood is there today, pleading for us and prevailing for us. The priest in the Tabernacle never spoke a word. All he did was PRESENT the blood, and that was enough. Perhaps there is a golden chalice in heaven where every drop of the precious blood is still in existence, just as pure, just as potent, just as fresh as two thousand years ago. The priest in the earthly Tabernacle needed to repeat the sprinkling again and again, and it is a significant fact that among all the pieces of the furniture of the Tabernacle there was no chair to be found. We read of the altar, the table, the candlestick and the Lord's Ark, but there is no mention of a chair in the Tabernacle of Israel. This fact simply signified that the work of the earthly priest who sprinkled the blood of animal sacrifice was never done. He could not sit down. His work was never finished. Of the great High Priest Jesus Christ, we read:

> But this man, after he had offered one sacrifice for sins forever, SAT DOWN on the right hand of God. For by one offering he hath perfected FOR EVER them that are sanctified (Hebrews 10:12, 14).

The blood has been shed — the incorruptible, eternal, divine, sinless, overcoming, precious blood. It availed then, and it avails now; and throughout all eternity it shall never lose its power.

Because of all this, the blood is called in Scripture by many descriptive names. "It is precious," says Peter. "It is incorruptible," says David. "It is overcoming blood," says John in Revelation *for they overcame him by the blood of the Lamb, and by the word of their testimony.* No wonder Satan hates the blood and will do anything to get rid of that power of the blood of Christ!

Today it is as true as in the day of Israel that there is no remission without the blood. Today the law has not changed its character; nor has the blood. The law still is the *ministration of death* (II Corinthians 3:7). It is still true that *cursed is everyone that continueth not in all things which are written in the book of the law to do them.* They that are of the works of the law are under the curse. *The letter killeth* (II Corinthians 3:6).

ONLY THE BLOOD

God said to Israel and to us, *When I see the blood, I will pass over you.* He did not say, "When I see your goodness, your morality, your works, your fervent religious worship, your earnestness in trying to keep the Ten Commandments or observe the Golden Rule, I will pass over you." No, it is simply this: *When I see the blood, I will pass over you.* Do you think that I have made too much of the blood; that I have overemphasized its importance? Listen, blood is mentioned in the Bible about SEVEN HUNDRED TIMES from Genesis to Revelation, and when we visualize the redeemed throng in heaven described in the book of the Revelation, we hear them singing, not about their goodness, not about how they have kept the law and been faithful, but this is the song:

> Unto him that loved us, and washed us from our sins in his own blood (Revelation 1:5).

IV

THE VIRGIN BIRTH

> Now the birth of Jesus Christ was on this wise: When as his mother Mary was espoused to Joseph, BEFORE THEY CAME TOGETHER, she was found with child of the Holy Ghost.
> Then Joseph her husband, being a just man, and not willing to make her a publick example, was minded to put her away privily.
> But while he thought on these things, behold, the angel of the Lord appeared unto him in a dream, saying, Joseph, thou son of David, fear not to take unto thee Mary thy wife for that WHICH IS CONCEIVED IN HER IS OF THE HOLY GHOST (Matthew 1:18-20).
> Now all this was done, that it might be fulfilled which was spoken of the Lord by the prophet, saying, Behold, a virgin shall be with child, and shall bring forth a son, and they shall call his name EMMANUEL, which being interpreted is, GOD WITH US (Matthew 1:22-23).

Passing strange, is it not, that with such a clear record

anyone can deny that *the Bible Teaches the Virgin Birth*. We can understand how men can reject the Bible record, but how men can say that the Bible does not teach the VIRGIN BIRTH is beyond conception.

The Bible teaches plainly that Jesus was conceived in the womb of a virgin Jewish mother by a supernatural act of the Holy Ghost, wholly and apart from any generation by a human father. This the Bible teaches so plainly that to the believer there is no room for doubt. The record cannot be mistaken by the careful and rigorous student of the Word.

JESUS SINLESS

The Bible teaches in addition that Jesus was a SINLESS man. Whereas all men from Adam to this day are born with Adam's sinful nature, and therefore are subject to the curse and eternal death, the Man Jesus was without sin and therefore DEATHLESS, until He took the sin of others upon Himself and died THEIR death.

God has made of ONE BLOOD ALL THE NATIONS of the earth. Even though Jesus, therefore, received His flesh, His body, from a sinful race, He could still be sinless as long as sinful blood was not in His body. God provided a way whereby Jesus could be perfectly human according to the flesh and yet not have the blood of sinful humanity. That was the problem solved by the virgin birth.

ORIGIN OF THE BLOOD

It is now definitely known that the blood which flows in an unborn babe's arteries and veins is not derived from the mother but is produced within the body of the foetus. Yet it is only after the sperm has entered the ovum and a foetus begins to develop that blood appears. As a very simple illustration of this, think of the egg of a hen. An unfertilized egg is simply an ovum on a much larger scale than the human ovum. You may incubate this unfertilized hen's egg, but it will never develop. It will dry up completely but no chick will result. But let that egg be fertilized by the introduction of the male sperm and incubation will bring to light the presence of LIFE IN AN

EMBRYO. After a few hours it visibly develops. In a little while red streaks occur, denoting the presence of BLOOD. And life is in the blood according to Scripture, for Moses says:

> For the life of the flesh is in the blood (Leviticus 17:11). For it is the life of all flesh; the blood of it is for the life thereof (Leviticus 17:14).

MOTHER'S BLOOD SEPARATE

It is unnecessary that a single drop of blood be given to the developing embryo in the womb of the mother. Such is the case according to scientists. The mother provides the foetus (the unborn developing infant) with the nutritive elements for the building of that little body in the secret of her womb, but all the blood which forms in it is formed in the embryo itself. From the time of conception to the time of birth of the infant not ONE SINGLE DROP OF BLOOD ever passes from mother to child. The placenta, that mass of temporary tissue known better as "afterbirth," forming the link between mother and child, is so constructed that although all the soluble nutritive elements such as proteins, fats, carbohydrates, salts, minerals and even antibodies pass freely from mother to child and the waste products of the child's metabolism are passed back to the mother's circulation, no actual interchange of a single drop of blood ever occurs normally. All the blood which is in that child is produced within the child itself. The mother contributes no blood at all.

TESTIMONY OF SCIENCE

Now for the sake of some readers who may doubt these statements let me quote from a few reliable authorities. In Howell's *Textbook of Physiology*, Second Edition, pages 885 and 886, I read:

> For the purpose of understanding its general functions it is sufficient to recall that the placenta consists essentially of vascular chorionic papillae from the foetus (the unborn child) bathed in the large blood spaces of the decidual membrane of the mother. The foetal and maternal blood DO NOT COME INTO ACTUAL CONTACT. THEY ARE SEPA-

RATED FROM EACH OTHER by the walls of the foetal blood vessels and the epithelial layers of the chorionic villae.

Or let me quote from Williams' *Practice of Obstetrics*, Third Edition, page 133:

The foetal blood in the vessels of the chorionic villae AT NO TIME GAINS ACCESS TO THE MATERNAL BLOOD in the intervillous spaces, BEING SEPARATED FROM ONE ANOTHER by the double layer of chorionic epithelium.

And from page 136 of the same recognized textbook I quote:

Normally there is no communication between the foetal blood and the maternal blood.

Now for the benefit of those of you who may be nurses, let me quote from a textbook which is familiar to you. I quote as follows from *Nurse's Handbook of Obstetrics* by Louise Zabriskie, R.N., Fifth Edition, page 75:

When the circulation of the blood begins in the embryo, it remains separate and distinct from that of the mother. All food and waste material which are interchanged between the embryo and the mother must pass through the blood vessel walls from one circulation to the other.

And from page 82 of the same book I quote:

The foetus receives its nourishment and oxygen from the mother's blood into its own through the medium of the placenta. The foetal heart pumps blood through the arteries of the umbilical cord into the placental vessels, which, looping in and out of the uterine tissue and lying in close contact with the uterine vessels, permit a diffusion, through their walls, of waste products from child to mother and of nourishment and oxygen from mother to child. As has been said, this interchange is effected by the process of osmosis, and there is no direct mingling of the two blood currents. In other words, no maternal blood actually flows to the foetus, nor is there any direct foetal blood flow to the mother.

GOD'S WONDERFUL PROVISION

How wonderfully God prepared for the virgin birth of His Son. When He created woman He made her so that no blood would be able to pass from her to her offspring. In order to produce a sinless man who would yet be the son of Adam,

God provided a way whereby that man would have a human body derived from Adam but have blood from a separate source. Some have tried to answer the question, "How could He be sinless and yet born of woman?" by making Mary the "Immaculate Virgin." That, however, does not answer the question of *how* JESUS was sinless.

It is plainly taught in Scripture that Jesus partook of human flesh without partaking of the effect of Adam's blood. In Hebrews 2:14 we read:

> Forasmuch then as the children are partakers of flesh and blood he also himself likewise took part of the same. . . .

You will notice that the "children," that is, the human children, are said to be partakers of FLESH and BLOOD, and then, speaking of Jesus, this verse says that He *himself likewise took part of the same.* The word "took part" as applying to Christ is an entirely different word from "partakers" as applied to the children. In the margin of my Bible, I read that the word translated "took part" implies "taking part in something outside one's self." The Greek word for partakers is KOYNONEHO and means "to share fully," so that all of Adam's children share fully in Adam's flesh and blood. When we read that Jesus "took part of the same" the word is METECHO which means "to take part but not all." The children take both flesh and blood of Adam but Christ took only part, that is, the flesh part, whereas the blood was the result of supernatural conception.

Jesus was a perfect human being after the flesh. He was of the seed of David according to the flesh, but blood is that part of a man which is the divine addition. In the creation of man, Adam's body was made from the dust of the earth, but God breathed into his nostrils the breath of life. Since life is in the blood, this act resulted in the formation of blood in Adam's body, but the first Adam's blood was corrupted and sin is in all mankind since God *hath made of one blood all nations.* In the last Adam and the second man, new and divine and sinless blood was produced in a body that was the seed of Adam and by this resulted in the production of —

DIVINE BLOOD

Conception by the Holy Ghost was the only way the virgin birth could be accomplished. Mary nourished the body of Jesus and He became the *seed of David according to the flesh*. The Holy Spirit contributed the blood of Jesus. It is sinless blood. It is divine blood. It is precious blood, for there has never been any other like it. It is —

INNOCENT BLOOD

I have betrayed the innocent blood, Judas confessed in Matthew 27:4. Our Lord was innocent. He became like unto us in all things — SIN only excepted; like unto us with ONE EXCEPTION — instead of being conceived by a human father, He was conceived by a DIVINE FATHER. As a result, biologically, He had DIVINE BLOOD, SINLESS BLOOD. Because this blood is sinless it is —

INCORRUPTIBLE BLOOD

Sin made human blood corruptible. Soon after death decay sets in, and it begins in the blood. That is why meat must be drained well of its blood. That is why embalmers place the embalming fluid in the blood. David said that *Jesus' body should not see corruption.* Though He was dead three days and three nights, His body did not corrupt. Because He was sinless they could not put Him to death but instead He laid down His life voluntarily that He might take it up again. He arose by His own power because death had no claim on HIM except the claim of others' sin, and when that was paid —

> Death cannot keep his prey —
> Jesus, my Saviour;
> He tore the bars away —
> Jesus, my Lord.
> Up from the grave He arose,
> With a mighty triumph o'er His foes.

Sinner, have you received this Saviour and have you been washed in HIS PRECIOUS BLOOD? If not, you are still under the curse and the awful sentence of death. Why not accept Him today and hear Him as He says:

God commendeth his love toward us, in that, while we were yet sinners, Christ died for us. Much more then, being now JUSTIFIED BY HIS BLOOD, we shall be saved from wrath through him (Romans 5:8, 9).

V

THE SANCTITY OF BLOOD

But flesh with the life thereof, which is the blood thereof, shall ye not eat (Genesis 9:4).

This is part of the very first command which God gave to man after the awful judgment of the Flood of Noah. After the wickedness of man had reached its peak in antediluvian days, God, in order to spare the human race from complete corruption, sent a great Flood upon the earth and destroyed all men except one family — the family of a man who by the grace of God had still remained *perfect in his generations*. With this new family on a cleansed and renewed earth, the Lord began a new chapter in the history of humanity. No sooner had God, however, released Noah from the Ark, than He gave him some instructions concerning his conduct, lest another judgment should fall upon them. Chief among these instructions was the commandment "EAT NO BLOOD." *But flesh with the life thereof, which is the blood thereof, shall ye not eat.* "EAT NO BLOOD," said God to man as he emerged on the new earth. Is there not here more than a mere suggestion that the Flood may have come in part as the result of man's disregard for the "sacredness of blood"?

We know that the earth was filled with violence, and the first overt sin committed after the fall was the sin of the shedding of Abel's innocent blood. This blood cried for vengeance from the ground. If that innocent blood called for vengeance in the Flood of Noah, shall God not also avenge the blood of those who today are dying because of the latter-day violence which is unquestionably in fulfillment of the words of our Lord when He said:

But as the days of Noe were, so shall also the coming of the Son of man be.

Yes, one of these days He is coming to put an end to the reign of terror on the earth, and, cleansing the world, by the judgment of the Tribulation of which the Flood was but a type, He will bring a kingdom of peace on another renewed and cleansed earth.

BLOOD IS SACRED

Because life is in the blood, and not in the flesh of God's creatures, He permitted man to eat FLESH, but it must be WITHOUT BLOOD. God was very insistent on this point. In giving the national dietary and ceremonial laws to Israel He repeated the prohibition of Genesis 9:4:

> Moreover ye shall eat no manner of blood, whether it be of fowl or of beast, in any of your dwellings. Whatsoever soul it be that eateth any manner of blood, even that soul shall be cut off from his people (Leviticus 7:26-27).

The same injunction is repeated at greater length in Leviticus 17. God said, "It is sin to eat any manner of blood." So serious was this sin that the transgressor was to be cut off from his people. Meat which had not been thoroughly drained of its blood was unfit for food, as well as all things strangled. Today, the orthodox Jew, at least, still remembers this prohibition, and will eat nothing but KOSHER meat, that is, meat which is without blood and which has been slaughtered according to the law. Every kosher meat market and every bit of kosher food is evidence of the sacredness of blood.

WE ARE UNDER GRACE

Now someone will say, "But we are under grace and that command was given to the Jews under the law." That objection carries no weight. God first gave the command to NOAH and NOAH WAS NOT UNDER THE LAW. He lived over a thousand years before the law of Moses was given on Mt. Sinai. More than that, after the law had been fulfilled in Christ and the age of grace ushered in, God is careful to let us know that this rule still holds: "EAT NO BLOOD." In the fifteenth chapter of Acts we have the record of the first general Church council at Jerusalem. A very vexing question had arisen in the early

Church after Paul and Barnabas had taken the Gospel to the Gentiles. The Jewish members of the early Church insisted that these Gentile believers become circumcised and demanded that thy keep the law. A bitter controversy arose and a meeting was called in Jerusalem to decide this question. Paul and Barnabas came down from Antioch for the meeting, and after much disputing they were sent back to the Gentile believers at Antioch with this message:

> Forasmuch as we have heard, that certain which went out from us have troubled you with words, subverting your souls, saying, Ye must be circumcised, and KEEP THE LAW: to whom we gave no such commandment (Acts 15:24).

Please notice carefully what the apostles said: "WE GAVE NO SUCH *Commandment.*" They denied that they ever taught that the Church was under the law or that Gentile believers had to be circumcised. Nineteen hundred years after, the Church is still vexed by these legalists who would make Jews out of us all, but the apostles emphatically declared that we are not under the law but under grace. The Christian does not keep the law because he MUST, but he serves God because of his gratitude for having been delivered from the law. Now notice the further instructions of the apostles:

> For it seemed good to the Holy Ghost, and to us, to lay upon you no greater burden than these necessary things;
> That ye abstain from meats offered to idols, and FROM BLOOD, AND FROM THINGS STRANGLED, and from fornication (Acts 15:28-29).

They were not under the law, but still they were to abstain from the eating of blood, not because they were under the law, but because of the SACREDNESS OF BLOOD, which is the life of all flesh. God gave the commandment to Noah a thousand years BEFORE the law. It held during the age of law and although the age of the law has passed, the commandment still holds today.

WHY NO BLOOD NOW?

God's commands are never arbitrary but always logical and reasonable. Many reasons can be found for abstaining from blood. We might mention the reasons of HEALTH and HYGIENE, but there are two reasons which stand out most prominently.

FIRST, the life is in the blood and LIFE is sacred. It was God's special gift and the effect of His own breath. Moses tells us, in Genesis, this fact:

> God formed man of the dust of the ground, and breathed into his nostrils the BREATH OF LIFE; and man became a living soul (Genesis 2:7).

Now follow closely the Biblical argument. Since life is in the blood, all flesh is lifeless without blood. Here was Adam formed from the dust — a lump of matter without life. God breathed into his nostrils and, lo, he became alive. Since the LIFE IS IN THE BLOOD, it was BLOOD which God added to that body when He BREATHED INTO HIM THE BREATH OF LIFE. Adam's body was of the earth, but his blood was DIRECTLY FROM GOD. God demands that we respect that fact, since it was God's own breath which filled all flesh with blood. To eat blood, therefore, is to insult the life of God for *the life . . . is in the blood*.

THE PRECIOUS BLOOD

There is a second and a more potent reason still. The blood was God's only purchase price of redemption. When man sinned, something happened to his blood, *for the life . . . is in the blood*. Instead of being incorruptible and, therefore, deathless blood, Adam's blood became corrupt through sin and became subject to death. To redeem this DEAD sinner, life must be again imparted. The only remedy for death is LIFE. This life is in the blood, and so blood must be furnished which is sinless and incorruptible. Now none of Adam's race could do this. For *in Adam all died. All have sinned and come short.* The angels could not furnish that blood for they are spirit beings and have neither flesh nor blood. There was only one, yes, ONLY ONE, who could furnish that blood: the virgin-born Son of God, with a human body, but sinless supernatural blood, imparted by the Holy Ghost. Elsewhere in this message we showed scientifically that every drop of blood in an infant's body is formed in the foetus separate from the mother, whereas the egg from the mother furnishes the beginning of the flesh of that little body. Jesus' body was of Mary; His blood was of the Holy Ghost. This sinless, supernatural blood was the only price of redemption God could accept, without violating the integrity of His holy nature. Death can only be banished by life. A blood transfusion must be performed and provided.

BLOOD TRANSFUSIONS

We hear much today about blood transfusions. Many lives have been saved by this procedure. In cases of hemorrhage and various diseases, the blood from healthy individuals is put in the veins of the suffering victim and death is cheated of its prey. The greatest of all "transfusions" is performed when a poor sinner, dead in trespasses and in sins, is saved by the blood of Christ the moment he believes. The only requisite is faith in the atoning blood.

BLOOD BANKS

We hear much, too, in these days about BLOOD BANKS. A "blood bank" is a storehouse for blood taken from healthy individuals for future use in the treatment of injured or sick persons. By adding certain preservatives to it, the blood taken from healthy individuals can be kept for future use in sterile containers. This preservative does not reduce the potency of the blood so that it can be used at some future date. Persons are asked to come to the hospital or laboratory to donate this blood. There, this blood is taken, treated and stored. In this way there is always an ample supply of blood for transfusion in any emergency. How wonderful are the findings of scientists! Today, you can give your blood which will a month from now save the life of some stranger a thousand miles away.

GOD'S BLOOD BANK

This is not one millionth as wonderful as what God did nineteen centuries ago. Then there was one Man who gave ALL His sinless blood on the Cross of Calvary. There a BLOOD BANK was opened and into that bank went the blood of the

Lord Jesus. It suits every type, avails for everyone and is free to all who will submit to its "transfusion" by the Holy Spirit. All you need do is to apply for it by FAITH. We must add chemicals to the blood in our blood banks to preserve it, and then it eventually deteriorates just the same, but no preservatives need be added to His precious blood, for it is INCORRUPTIBLE and sinless blood. Not one drop of that blood was lost or wasted. It is INCORRUPTIBLE.

> Forasmuch as ye know that ye were not redeemed with CORRUPTIBLE THINGS, as silver and gold. . . . But with the precious BLOOD of Christ, as of a lamb without blemish and without spot (I Peter 1:18, 19).

Hallelujah for the blood! Reader, do you know that blood is as fresh today as it ever was and always will be? It cannot perish. There is a hymn which goes something like this:

> Upon the Cross His blood was spilt,
> A ransom for our sins and guilt.

That is not true. Jesus' blood was not "spilled." Spilling is the result of an accident. The death of Christ was no accident. He laid down His life and voluntarily shed His precious blood that we might live.

Oh, sinner, won't you appropriate that precious blood Now! There is nothing else which can wash you clean from the guilt and the power of sin. Receive it today and be saved.

You believers who have been grieving over your sins, remember —

> If we confess our sins, he is faithful and just to forgive us our sins, and to CLEANSE us from all unrighteousness (I John 1:9).

TRUST HIM NOW

> There is a fountain filled with blood,
>   Drawn from Immanuel's veins;
> And sinners, plunged beneath that flood,
>   Lose all their guilty stains.

CHAPTER 2

THE CHEMISTRY OF CONSCIENCE

A great deal of interest has been awakened in an invention of recent date called the "lie detector." It is a scientific instrument which is said to possess the power to detect whether a man or woman is telling the truth. It has been subjected widely to rigid scientific tests and is declared by many criminologists and psychologists to be accurate and dependable. By others it is discredited, and in many courts it has not as yet been endorsed.

The whole subject is still in its infancy and the doubts in many minds concerning its practicability are due to the fact that it has not been sufficiently used in actual cases and investigators have not been able to make proper tests. We believe that the invention of the "lie detector" is the beginning of an unlimited field of research in the matter of criminology and psychology. It can easily be proved to be scientific and based upon well-known and recognized physiological and psychological principles.

The "Lie Detector" in the Bible

The Bible records the use of the first scientific "lie detector" and whereas the "lie detectors" now in use in the world are of very recent invention, the one described by Moses in the Word is ALMOST FOUR THOUSAND YEARS OLD. You will find the record in the fifth chapter of Numbers, and a study of it will form the subject matter of this message.

> If any man's wife go aside, and commit a trespass against him,
> And a man lie with her carnally, and IT BE HID FROM THE EYES OF HER HUSBAND, and be kept close, and she be defiled, and THERE BE NO WITNESS AGAINST HER, neither she be taken with the manner [in the act];

And the spirit of jealousy come upon him, and he be JEALOUS [suspicious] of his wife, and she be not defiled:

Then shall the man bring his wife unto the priest and he shall bring her offering for her, the tenth part of an ephah of barley meal; he shall pour no oil upon it, nor put frankincense thereon; for it is an offering of jealousy, an offering of memorial, BRINGING INIQUITY TO REMEMBRANCE.

And the priest shall bring her near and SET HER BEFORE THE LORD . . . AND UNCOVER THE WOMAN'S HEAD [thus taking her glory away], and put the offering of memorial in her hands, which is the JEALOUSY OFFERING: and the priest shall have in his hand the BITTER WATER that causeth the CURSE:

And the priest shall charge her by an oath, and say unto the woman, If no man have lain with thee, and if thou hast not gone aside to uncleanness with another instead of thy husband, be thou free from this bitter water that causeth the curse: But if thou hast gone aside to another instead of thy husband, and if thou be defiled, and some man have lain with thee beside thine husband:

Then the priest shall charge the woman with an oath of cursing, and the priest shall say unto the woman, The Lord make thee a curse and an oath among thy people, when the Lord doth make THY THIGH TO ROT, AND THY BELLY TO SWELL;

And this water that causeth the curse shall go into thy bowels, to make thy belly to swell, and thy thigh to rot: and the woman shall say, AMEN, AMEN.

And the priest shall write these curses in a book, and he shall blot them out with the bitter water:

And he shall cause the woman to drink the bitter water that causeth the curse; and the water that causeth the curse shall enter into her, and become bitter.

Then the priest shall take the jealousy offering out of the woman's hand, and shall wave the offering before the Lord, and offer it upon the altar:

And the priest shall take an handful of the offering, even the memorial thereof, and burn it upon the altar, and afterward shall cause the woman to drink the water.

AND WHEN HE HATH MADE HER TO DRINK THE WATER, THEN IT SHALL COME TO PASS, THAT, IF SHE BE DEFILED, AND HAVE DONE TRESPASS AGAINST HER HUSBAND, THAT THE WATER THAT CAUSETH THE CURSE SHALL ENTER INTO HER, AND BECOME BITTER, AND HER BELLY SHALL SWELL, AND HER THIGH SHALL ROT: AND THE WOMAN SHALL BE A CURSE AMONG HER PEOPLE.

AND IF THE WOMAN BE NOT DEFILED, BUT BE CLEAN;
THEN SHE SHALL BE FREE, AND SHALL CONCEIVE SEED.

IS THIS TEST SCIENTIFIC?

We know that this record is the inspired Word of the living God and no true child of His doubts for a moment that the test really worked when it was applied. But the question is: Was this a test that depended upon the SUPERNATURAL for its working, and was it one of those miracles which served only for a season? Or is there a SCIENTIFIC BASIS and foundation for the test apart from the miraculous and will it work today?

We believe, although we would not detract a whit from the miraculous in the Bible, that this test did not depend upon a miracle at all but was a normal physical test which depended upon the ordinary physical and psychological functions of the body. We believe that, if we KNEW THE IDENTITY OF THE BITTER HERB which Moses used, the SAME TEST WOULD WORK TODAY. Recent discoveries in the realm of physiological chemistry and the psychological effects on the body will greatly strengthen this position.

PHYSIOLOGY AND PSYCHOLOGY

The "lie detector," as we have it today, depends upon the fact that certain psychological and emotional changes react upon the tissues of the body and cause specific changes in the physical functions of the organism. A normal emotion resulting in a peaceful consciousness of innocence will produce either no change or a different reaction. An abnormal emotional state caused by telling a lie, especially under oath, and with the danger of detection, will cause certain other changes in the muscles and secretions, which, when tested or measured, can tell us whether there is present an ABNORMAL PSYCHOLOGY caused by a sense of guilt or fear or a NORMAL EMOTIONAL change brought about by the consciousness of INNOCENCE.

Investigators have discovered that when a man tells a lie certain emotional changes take place which react upon and affect the heart and the blood vessel and cause a change in the blood pressure. When a man is telling the truth this change is absent, but when he is under the abnormal emotional pressure of telling a lie the change is noted on the instrument which records the fluctuations in the pressure of the circulation. A little thought, I am sure, will convince anyone that this is neither impossible nor contrary to ordinary physical facts.

BLUSHING

Blushing is a reddening of the skin, especially of the face and neck, caused by a sudden dilation of the peripheral blood vessels, and is accompanied by a sensation of heat. This PHYSICAL CHANGE is caused by an EMOTIONAL OR PSYCHOLOGICAL stimulation. The emotion of EMBARRASSMENT causes a physical change in the body. The emotion of fear causes the face to TURN WHITE — the very opposite physical reaction of embarrassment and blushing. Great EXPECTATION or surprise produces "tachycardia" (rapid heart). Increased respiration and deep sighing result from other emotions.

Sudden surprises and fright may cause VOMITING. Anguish may cause one to sweat. Fits of anger often result in apoplexy and death because of the sudden increase in the blood pressure which they produce. In the realm of "hysteria" we have an inexhaustible field. In the realm of sex life we have another realm which has scarcely been entered by modern science. But we trust that the above examples are sufficient to PROVE THAT EMOTIONAL CHANGES AND PSYCHOLOGICAL STIMULI DO AFFECT THE HEART, BLOOD VESSELS, SECRETIONS, and, in fact, every organ and tissue in the human body. The mere THOUGHT of food is sufficient to cause the "mouth to water," which, of course, is simply the evidence that the salivary glands have been aroused to secretory activity by a pleasant thought.

THE JEALOUSY OFFERING

The test prescribed in Numbers 5 is based on the preceding scientific facts. They were given to Moses by inspiration and anticipated modern science by four thousand years. This particular "lie detector" which Moses used utilized the principles in use today. The subject MUST KNOW that the test is to be applied. Usually it is administered under OATH. He must be impressed with the certainty of the results and the dire consequences if he is found guilty of the crime and of lying under oath.

The story as we have it in Numbers 5 is very simple. In the case of a man who had become SUSPICIOUS of his wife and was jealous of her, the following procedure was inaugurated. If there was no witness to the sin and no direct evidence was available, the woman was taken to the priest and her head covering removed. A jealousy offering was brought to impress the woman with the gravity of the situation which required an offering. It was probably designed to induce her to confess her guilt (in case she was guilty) and accept the offering for her. If she did not confess, she was PUT UNDER OATH. The priest then told her in great detail just what would happen. He was going to give her a drink of bitter water. It was water containing some kind of an herb or drug and she was informed by the priest that if she was guilty and lied about it, this potion would act as a violent poison, causing peritonitis and gangrene and, ultimately, death. If she was guiltless, it would not affect her. All this was very, very impressively done so that the person being tested could not fail to realize the importance of telling the truth. You can imagine the nervous condition of the individual after this ordeal.

THE TEST

Once more the priest stated the facts to the woman. He described the consequences which would follow if she lied and the freedom from penalty if she told the truth. Then the woman repeated the oath and said, "AMEN, AMEN" ("So be it"). She was then given the bitter cup with its testing drug, and invariably the test was successful. If she was guilty, the dreaded inflammation and gangrene resulted, and if she was not guilty, nothing serious ensued.

We do not know what the drug was which Moses used. If we did we should have something far better and surer than the modern lie detector. But, like the Egyptian formula for embalming and other arts, the formula is lost and we may never find it. But the scientific basis is not in any way undermined by our ignorance of the identity of the drug.

It is well known that certain emotions and nervous disturbances result in a change in the secretions and functions of the body. A baby has the colic because the mother had a FIT OF ANGER. There were produced in the body of the mother certain ptomaines or alkaloidal poisons as the result of her disturbed emotions and these were transmitted to the babe in the mother's milk. We know that in the same way emotions and nervous disorders result in a poisoning of the system and the throwing off of products of incomplete combustion. Many cases of so-called "dyspepsia" are of purely nervous origin, yet there is a chemical change in the secretions of the stomach. Many cases of autointoxication result from the same cause.

DISHONESTY POISONS

The telling of a lie causes the secretion or formation of certain poisons which alone may be harmless but which when COMBINED WITH OTHER POISON become fatal. When the two are brought together the result is as described in Numbers 5. Moses knew this. We cannot appreciate what Moses knew because we have barely begun to investigate the startling effects produced by the mind and emotions. The various cults and isms have obscured a few of these phenomena, and this accounts, I am sure, for many of their reputed "cures." Correction of the EMOTIONAL STATE may cure what appears to be a "physical" disease.

When, therefore, an individual was put under oath and under severe conscious strain and he STILL LIED, the system would secrete certain bodies or fluids which when combined with the BITTER DRUG in the cup would act as a violent poison and cause the symptom described. When the emotions were normal, as to honesty at least, these particular bodies were not secreted and the bitter cup could be quaffed with impunity.

We know that generally it is not the elements themselves which are poisonous; usually the particular combination in which these elements occur determines their lethal character. Carbon dioxide (CO_2) is a harmless gas but if we make the proportion of the two elements one of carbon and one of oxygen we have one of the most poisonous and deadly gases known; viz., carbon monoxide. Carbon, oxygen and hydrogen in the right proportions and combinations will make sugar or starch — A FOOD — but if we change the proportion of the same elements slightly the result is ALCOHOL — A POISON. Two atoms of hydrogen and one of oxygen form water — A GOOD DRINK — but the same elements in the proportion of two atoms of hydrogen and two of oxygen form HYDROGEN PEROXIDE — AN ANTISEPTIC.

Chemistry is replete with numerous examples of this fact that two or more harmless elements or combinations of elements when combined in a different way or with other elements may form a very poisonous substance. The BITTER water formed No POISONOUS combination with the normal secretions occasioned by an emotional sense of innocence, but produced JUST THE OPPOSITE RESULT when combined with the ABNORMAL SECRETIONS caused by the emotionally perverted stimulus of guilt.

Will anyone dare say that the Bible is not a scientific Book and that Moses was in error? Certainly to do so is to reveal one's ignorance.

ITS APPLICATION

However, the fact that this was a scientific "lie detector" does not exhaust its meaning. All these laws and regulations looked beyond the immediate use and carry a lesson for all of us; for after all, GOD DOES NOT NEED A LIE DETECTOR. It is only men, because of their inability to look into the human heart, who need these things. But it was God Himself who said, *Out of [the heart] are the issues of life.* We wonder just how much is wrapped up in that phrase OUT *of [the heart] are the* ISSUES *of life.* He knows the heart. Nothing is hid from His sight. He knows all, and there is a day coming when He will unveil all which has not come under the covering blood of the Lord Jesus Christ.

Oh, sinner, you may hide your sin and your guilt by careful and clever hypocrisy. The darkness may cover your sin and you may say, "No man knoweth," but remember that GOD KNOWS. He sees your heart and knows your guilt. He stands ready with the offering and bids you come for cleansing and for pardon. He offers, today, the Lord Jesus. Will you accept Him? If you do HE WILL SAVE you and take all your GUILT AWAY, and deliver you from the wrath of hell forever. BUT if you will not — then your blood shall be upon your own head. The time will soon be here when the judgment shall sit and God *will bring to light the hidden things of darkness, and will make manifest the counsels of the hearts* (I Corinthians 4:5).

> For though thou wash thee with nitre, and take thee much sope, yet thine iniquity is marked before me, saith the Lord God (Jeremiah 2:22).
> For there is nothing covered, that shall not be revealed; neither hid, that shall not be known.
> Therefore whatsoever ye have spoken in darkness shall be heard in the light; and that which ye have spoken in the ear in closets shall be proclaimed upon the house-tops (Luke 12:2, 3).
> For every one that doeth evil hateth the light, neither cometh to the light, lest his deeds should be reproved.
> But he that doeth truth cometh to the light, that his deeds may be made manifest, that they are wrought in God (John 3:20, 21).

CHAPTER 3

THE CHEMISTRY OF CALVARY

THE LINE OF THE BLOOD

Through the Bible from cover to cover runs an unbroken, continuous scarlet red stream of blood from an atoning sacrifice. It begins in the sacrifice spoken of in Genesis 3:21 where we read that God made coats of skin through the sacrifice of an innocent animal, that Adam and Eve might be covered. It runs in a continuous stream through the sacrifices of Noah, Abraham, Exodus, Leviticus and the whole Old Testament system until it bursts forth in the supreme sacrifice of Calvary and runs on in an ever-increasing and widening course through the years and will flow on through the countless ages of eternity. The song in eternity will be: *Unto him who loved us, and washed us from our sins in his own blood.*

THE FIRST SACRIFICE

The first recorded sacrifice in the Bible is in Genesis 3:21.

> Unto Adam also and to his wife did the Lord God make coats of skins, and clothed them.

This verse teaches us that after man had sinned, God supplied an animal and shed its blood, and used the skin as a covering for Adam and Eve's nakedness. In this one brief record we have the plan of all subsequent Scriptural sacrifice. We have in the Bible a law which we call the "LAW OF FIRST MENTION": When applied to this particular verse, it gives us the key to the meaning of sacrifice in the Word of God. This law of first mention might be stated as follows:

THE FIRST USE OF A WORD, A PHRASE OR INCIDENT IN THE

BIBLE GIVES THE KEY TO ITS EXACT MEANING EVERYWHERE ELSE IN THE WORD OF GOD.

Apply this law to Genesis 3:21 and we find that it teaches three things:

First: SALVATION MUST BE OF THE LORD.

Second: IT MUST BE BY THE DEATH OF AN INNOCENT SUBSTITUTE.

Third: IT MUST BE BY BLOOD.

Every acceptable sacrifice must meet these three conditions. It must not be man's work but God's work, not man's provision but God's provision; not the fig leaves of man's own righteousness but bloody skins of God's providing. Every true sacrifice mentioned in Scripture has three essential features. We find that Abel's sacrifice met the condition of Genesis 3:21 whereas Cain's did not. Cain brought a sacrifice of his own. It was not the substitute of another. Abel, on the other hand, brought a lamb, an innocent substitute, in his place, and was justified before God in the shedding of its blood; namely, its death.

OTHER INSTANCES

This same plan holds true in every sacrifice mentioned in the Old Testament. Noah took one of the clean animals which God had provided by commanding him to take seven instead of two, and thus it was the sacrifice of God's provision. It was the death of an innocent substitute and acceptable by blood. As we read in Genesis 22, when Abraham was ready to slay his son, God showed him a ram caught by its horns in the thicket. Again God provided a sacrifice, and the sacrifice was an innocent substitute and accomplished by the shedding of blood. All through Leviticus we have the same plan clearly evident in the Burnt Offering, the Peace Offering, the Sin Offering and the Trespass Offering. All through the Old Testament this scarlet line runs unbroken until it bursts at the Cross in the antitypical sacrifice of the Lamb of God. He fulfilled the three requirements of an acceptable sacrifice:

1. It must be God's gift. *For God so loved the world, that he gave his only begotten Son, that whosoever believeth*

in him should not perish, but have everlasting life (John 3:16).

2. It must be by the death of an innocent sacrifice. *Who did no sin, neither was guile found in his mouth: who, when he was reviled, reviled not again; when he suffered, he threatened not; but committed himself to him that judgeth righteously: who his own self bare our sins in his own body on the tree, that we, being dead to sin, should live unto righteousness: by whose stripes ye were healed* (I Peter 2:22-24).

3. It must be by blood. *Forasmuch as ye know that ye were not redeemed with corruptible things, as silver and gold, from your vain conversation received by tradition from your fathers; but with the precious blood of Christ, as of a lamb without blemish and without spot: who verily was foreordained before the foundation of the world, but was manifest in these last times for you* (I Peter 1:18-20).

That stream is still flowing and will avail through all eternity.

> Dear dying Lamb, Thy precious blood
> Shall never lose its power,
> Till all the ransomed Church of God
> Be saved, to sin no more.

THE NECESSITY OF THE BLOOD

The reason why the Lord must demand blood for the atonement of sin lies in the nature of God and in the nature of sin. Since God is perfectly and unimpeachably holy, sin can never be passed over without a satisfaction of the justice of God and since sin is rebellion against an infinite God, the Highest Being, only the greatest and the highest price can be accepted as an atonement for sin. God gave unto Israel a holy, a perfect and a just law upon Mount Sinai.

Disobedience to this law demanded the greatest penalty in payment. It was for this reason that God gave in the Tabernacle Service the Ark of the Covenant in the Holy of Holies. You will remember that this Ark consisted of an oblong box made of acacia wood and covered with beaten gold. In this Ark reposed the law which had been broken by Israel when Moses was upon the Mount. The broken law demanded the eternal damnation of Israel, but God had made a provision and so planned the Mercy Seat of beaten gold to cover this broken law.

Once a year, on the Day of Atonement, the high priest took the blood of the animal sacrifice, God's provision, from the Altar of Burnt Offering and sprinkled it on the Mercy Seat. The broken law was then covered by the blood of a sacrifice. God was appeased; and atonement had been made. His justice was satisfied. His mercy could flow out unhindered to His erring people.

To look upon the broken law without blood is to face wrath. God said, *When I see the blood, I will pass over you.* To remove the blood from God's righteous judgment is to invite certain destruction.

BETH-SHEMESH

As an illustration of the above, we have the record in I Samuel 6 of the Ark of the Covenant being taken captive by the Philistines. During the time that the Ark was in the possession of the Philistines, God sent upon them divers diseases and plagues. *The hand of the Lord was against the city with a very great destruction,* we read in I Samuel 5:9. They were plagued with a very painful and rare disease. As a result the lords of the Philistines called for the diviners and soothsayers and inquired into the cause of this dire calamity. These men rightly diagnosed the case and informed the lords that it was because of the Ark of the Covenant of Israel that was in their midst.

Accordingly they devised a very unique scheme. They decided that a pair of young kine who had recently given birth to calves should be harnessed to a new wagon upon which the Ark was to be placed, together with some golden emerods and golden mice, and headed in the direction of the land of Israel. If the two cows went in a straight line away from their young, it would be an indication that the Ark was the cause of their distress. But if the cows would refuse to leave their calves and turn around, it would indicate that the Ark was not the cause of the plagues and the sickness.

The result was that the cows, contrary to nature, went in

a straight line to the land of Israel and came to the city of the Levites, Beth-shemesh. Upon the arrival of the Ark of the Covenant in Beth-shemesh, there was great rejoicing and in the course of their hilarious celebration the men of Beth-shemesh inadvertently lifted up the Mercy Seat to see whether the contents of the Ark had been disturbed by the Philistines. Moved by curiosity, they removed for a moment the bloody covering from the Ark of God. For only a brief minute they looked upon the broken law of God without the blood, and we read the tragic result in I Samuel 6:19:

> And he smote the men of Beth-shemesh, because they had looked into the ark of the Lord, even he smote of the people fifty thousand and threescore and ten men: and the people lamented, because the Lord had smitten many of the people with a great slaughter.

To look upon the broken law of God without blood means certain death. The only sacrifice must be by blood.

Another striking illustration which will set forth this truth in a clear way is in the atonement which Moses offered after the people had broken God's law by the making of the golden calf at Mount Sinai. Moses and Joshua had been on the mountain for forty days and forty nights. During their absence Israel had given them up as dead. They demanded that Aaron construct a god to lead them on the way. The result was the manufacture of the golden calf. When Moses descended from the Mount with the Tablets of the Testimony in his hand he found that Israel had already broken the first two of God's commands and had already placed themselves under the curse of God. Moses knew that nothing but a blood atonement could avert disaster for the children of Israel, and so we find a very unique account of Moses' sacrifice for Israel's sin. He said to them in essence: "You have sinned a great sin. You ought to die, yet I am going to bring an atonement unto God. I don't know whether this thing will work. I am not sure this will avail, but I am going to try it in order that you may be saved and spared." We have the whole story in the record in Exodus 32.

> And he took the calf which they had made, and burnt it in

> the fire, and ground it to powder, and strawed it upon the
> water, and made the children of Israel drink of it (Exodus
> 32:20).

You will notice from this verse that Moses took the golden
calf and —

1. Melted it.
2. Ground it to powder.
3. Put it on the water.
4. Made the children of Israel drink of it.

In Deuteronomy 9 we have the same record a bit more
elaborately.

> And I took your sin, the calf which ye had made, and burnt
> it with fire, and stamped it, and ground it very small, even
> until it was as small as dust: and I cast the dust thereof into
> the brook that descended out of the mount (Deut. 9:21).

You will notice that Moses goes into greater detail here and
you will note that six things are mentioned concerning the
golden calf:

1. He melted it.
2. He stamped it.
3. He ground it.
4. He ground it again.
5. He put it into the brook.
6. He made the children of Israel drink it.

Then, as we shall see in a moment, he took some of the water
out of the brook and presented it to God for the blood atonement of the sins of Israel.

Moses' Knowledge of Chemistry

It is very evident from this record that Moses had a super-
naturally-given knowledge of the science of chemistry. You may
have wondered why Moses took the calf and submitted it to
the melting, pounding, grinding and suspension. The result was
a suspension which became a vivid type of the blood of the
Lord Jesus Christ.

In chemistry we speak of three kinds of mixtures They are
as follows:

1. A MECHANICAL MIXTURE. If I drop a piece of metallic

gold in water, no solution occurs. The gold is intact and remains in the water. Pure gold is insoluble in water.

2. A SUSPENSION or EMULSION. Finely divided particles of a metallic substance may, by the addition of another chemical, be suspended in water. There is no solution. The finely ground particles are merely suspended in the water. We call this an EMULSION.

3. A CHEMICAL SOLUTION. If I take a teaspoonful of sugar and put it into a glass of water, the sugar will not mix or be suspended, but will enter into a solution so that the result will be an increase in weight but not an increase in volume. The sugar dissolves and the atoms take up their place in the interatomic spaces in the water. This is a SOLUTION.

GOLD INSOLUBLE IN WATER

"Gold is insoluble in water, being nineteen times heavier with a specific gravity of 19.5. In fine powder it assumes a colloidal condition, and added to water results in a coloration that appears to be solution. As the particles are made finer the bulk is greatly increased and acquires an "apparent" specific gravity permitting its suspension in water, giving the liquid a deep red color. Scientific records state that "colloidal" gold in water is a rose-red color when the particles are of 10 micron size in a dilution of 1 to 100,000 (10 microns equal .0003937 or 0.0004 inches). From this you will see that gold in "dust" size will color water as "blood", which means that this calf of gold need not have been very large to color sufficient water blood-red to furnish drinks to at least two or more million people. COLLOIDAL gold can be made in many ways but the method of Moses is the best under the circumstances in the wilderness. The burning removed the impurities; the stamping (beating) reduced it to thin sheets because of the ductability of gold. Gold leaf can be made so thin that it requires about 280,000 to make one inch. Sheets as thin as 00.000004 inch have made. Then the grinding becomes easy, and further information proves that Moses ground it very fine, as fine as dust, reducing it to the size of colloidal gold; this cast into the brook would make the water blood-red. It was non-toxic (impurities having been burned out) and was inhibitory to germ life. The resultant waters would be blood-red and possess purifying qualities. All of this was a fitting type of the blood of the Lord Jesus Christ."*

MOSES' OFFERING

This blood-red solution was taken by Moses before the Lord and presented to Him as an atonement for their sin. We have the record clearly given in Exodus 32:30, 31 and 32.

> And it came to pass on the morrow, that Moses said unto the people, Ye have sinned a great sin: and now I will go up unto the Lord; peradventure I shall make an atonement for your sin.
> And Moses returned unto the Lord, and said, Oh, this people have sinned a great sin, and have made them gods of gold.
> Yet now, if thou wilt forgive their sin — ; and if not, blot me, I pray thee, out of thy book which thou hast written.

Here Moses presented his atonement, saying, *Peradventure I shall make an atonement for your sin.* The Lord saw the blood-red solution, a fit type of the blood of the Lord Jesus Christ. His wrath was averted, His justice appeased, and His love again flowed forth.

APPROPRIATION

One other thing remains to be said concerning this blood. Although Moses made an atonement and God accepted it, only those who by faith appropriated it were saved. The others died. This is very strongly suggested in the record in Exodus 32:26-28:

> Then Moses stood in the gate of the camp, and said, Who is on the Lord's side? let him come unto me. And all the sons of Levi gathered themselves together under him.
> And he said unto them, Thus saith the Lord God of Israel, Put every man his sword by his side, and go in and out from gate to gate throughout the camp, and slay every man his brother, and every man his companion, and every man his neighbour. And the children of Levi did according to the word of Moses: and there fell of the people that day about three thousand men.

* From a personal letter received from William Schepp of Schepp Laboratories.

Although it is not explicitly stated, it is plainly suggested that the three thousand men who were slain by the swords of the Levites on that day were those who refused to stoop down and drink of the crimson brook that descended out of the Mount. Those who accepted God's provision through the molten golden calf were saved. Those who rejected were lost. Although it is true that Christ died for the sin of the whole world and He tasted death for every man, it still remains a fact that only those who by faith appropriate His provision will be saved.

Nineteen hundred years ago on Calvary's Cross the fountain was opened in the wounded side of the dying Christ. From that day to this a stream has been flowing into which all who will may plunge and receive remission of sins and eternal salvation. To accept the blood is to live. To reject it is to die. What have you done with the blood of the slain Lamb? In heaven today there is a resurrected Christ who paid for the sin of the world on Calvary's Cross, waiting to give life, peace, joy and victory to all who will stoop down and drink and live.

> I heard the voice of Jesus say,
> "Come unto Me and rest;
> Lay down, thou weary one, lay down
> Thy head upon My breast."
> I came to Jesus as I was,
> Weary and worn and sad;
> I found in Him a resting place,
> And He has made me glad.
> I heard the voice of Jesus say,
> "Behold, I freely give
> The living water; thirsty one,
> Stoop down and drink, and live."
> I came to Jesus, and I drank
> Of that life-giving stream;
> My thirst was quenched, my soul revived,
> And now I live in Him.

CHAPTER 4

THE CHEMISTRY OF LIGHT

"GOD IS LIGHT" (I John 1:5).

There was a time when there was no time. Before time began, God was complete and all-sufficient in His eternal pre-existence. He was perfect in Himself — perfect in all His attributes, virtues and graces. When He created the universe by the word of His power, He added nothing to His being or to His glory, or to His majesty. God's glory is no greater since the creation than before. His great creation only serves as an exhibition of His infinite majesty, power, glory, wisdom and providence.

God created all things for His own glory. In order that He may be appreciated in His infinite personality, He has revealed His majesty and glory to His creatures in various ways. Let it therefore be understood at the beginning of this message that creation added nothing to the glory of God. To glorify God does not mean to add anything to His glory, but rather to reflect, show forth and disseminate the glory which He has always had.

THREE AVENUES OF REVELATION

1. Through NATURE. From creation man is able to learn a great deal about God. David tells us in Psalm 19:1-3:

> The heavens declare the glory of God; and the firmament sheweth his handywork.
> Day unto day uttereth speech, and night unto night sheweth knowledge.
> There is no speech nor language, where their voice is not heard.

From this passage it is clear that we can learn something

about the glory and wisdom of God from nature. In Romans 1:18 to 20 Paul tells us:

> For the wrath of God is revealed from heaven against all ungodliness and unrighteousness of men, who hold the truth in unrighteousness.
> Because that which may be known of God is manifest in them; for God hath shewed it unto them.
> For the invisible things of him from the creation of the world are clearly seen, being understood by the things that are made, even his eternal power and Godhead; so that they are without excuse.

This is the simplest revelation of God.

2. Through the printed WORD OF GOD. In the Bible we have a progression in revelation. In addition to the revelation of nature, we learn to know God from the Word as a God of love, a God of grace, a God of mercy, justice and truth. In it we have the plan of salvation. In this Book we not only have the revelation of our lost condition and the fact of sin and distress in the world but the great truth of redemption through blood and the sacrifice of Another.

3. In the PERSON OF CHRIST. The highest revelation we have is in the Person of the Lord Jesus Christ, one of the Persons of the Trinity. In Colossians 1:15-17 we read:

> Who is the image of the invisible God, the firstborn of every creature:
> For by him were all things created, that are in heaven, and that are in earth, visible and invisible, whether they be thrones, or dominions, or principalities, or powers: all things were created by him, and for him;
> And he is before all things, and by him all things consist.

Again in Colossians 1:19 we read:

> For it pleased the Father that in him should all fulness dwell.

In Colossians 2:9 we read:

> For in him dwelleth all the fulness of the Godhead bodily.

Jesus Himself said, *He that hath seen me hath seen the Father*. In Hebrews 1:1-3 we read:

> God, who at sundry times and in divers manners spake in

time past unto the fathers by the prophets, Hath in these last days spoken unto us by his Son, whom he hath appointed heir of all things, by whom also he made the worlds; Who being the brightness of his glory, and the EXPRESS IMAGE OF HIS PERSON, and upholding all things by the word of his power, when he had by himself purged our sins, sat down on the right hand of the Majesty on high.

God is invisible as a Spirit. He cannot be seen. Only in Christ do we see God.

REVEALED BY ATTRIBUTES

God has pleased to make Himself known to us through His attributes revealed in the Person of Christ. We can classify these attributes in various ways, but for our present purpose we shall divide them into two groups.

1. Those attributes which tell us something about God and His characteristics, such as His mercy, His justice, His long-suffering, His holiness, etc.

2. Those attributes which describe His Being, the very essence of His character, WHAT HE IS. These are, among others, as follows:

a. God is LIFE.

b. God is LOVE.

c. God is LIGHT.

My present message has to do with the last one of these three.

WHAT IS LIGHT?

The Bible says that God is light. Light is invisible. No one has ever seen pure light. No one has ever seen sunlight. The things which we really see are the objects which the light reveals. As I write these words, I see a desk, books, telephone, hat, bookcase, chairs and others objects which are revealed by the light. I do not see the light. If these objects were not here, I would see nothing. Those who have gone up in stratosphere flights many miles above the earth tell us there is complete darkness where there are no objects to be seen. *God is light, and in him is no darkness at all.* We cannot see God. Only as we see the light reflected in the Person of Jesus Christ do we see Him.

PROPERTIES OF THE SUN

We have just stated that pure light is invisible. The source of our light upon this earth comes, with the exception of a certain amount of cosmic radiation and the bit of starlight that reaches the earth, from the sun as the center of our solar system. It is just in recent years that we have begun to appreciate the wonders of sunlight. We shall quote one or two paragraphs appearing recently in *Therapeutic Notes*.

> To arrive at an intelligent attitude toward the effects of sunlight, one must start with certain fundamental physical data. The sun is approximately 93 million miles from the earth. Its diameter is 110 times that of the earth, and its volume 1,300 thousand times that of the earth. Because of difference in density, however, the sun's mass is only about 330 thousand times that of the earth.
>
> The sun's brightness is so great it is difficult to express intelligibly in terms of earthly objects. The intense calcium light or an electric arc light interposed between the eye and the sun will look like a black spot on the disc. The sun is nearly four times brighter than the 'crater' or brightest part of an electric arc.
>
> The heat of the sun is prodigious. The temperature at the surface is probably not less than 16,000 degrees F. One square meter of the sun's surface radiates enough heat to generate 100,000 horsepower continuously. Even at our vast distance the sun's heat received by the earth is powerful enough to melt annually a layer of ice more than 100 feet in thickness. That portion of the sun's radiation which is received by the earth represents only 1/2,220 millionth part of the total light and heat radiated.

God is light, and in him is no darkness at all. The highest development of man's scientific attainment, the calcium arc light, still is a black spot in comparison with the brightness of the sun. The highest attainments of man — his best works, his best efforts, great as they may be from a human standpoint — are yet, in the light of God's perfect standards of holiness and His demands of perfection, merely black spots. Or, as Scripture puts it, *filthy rags.* How futile, how fruitless and foolish are all of man's efforts to seek to attain unto righteousness by his own works, by his own efforts and by his own endeavors.

The highest attainment and effort of man must ever remain a black spot in comparison with the holy demands of a living God. *God is light and in him is no darkness at all.*

THREE KINDS OF RAYS

A scientific analysis of sunlight reveals that it consists of three kinds of rays:

1. *Chemical rays or actinic.* These rays are invisible and can neither be felt nor seen.

2. *Light rays.* These rays can be seen but are never felt.

3. *Heat rays.* These rays are felt but never seen.

GOD *is light, and in him is no darkness at all.* We know that the Godhead consists of Three Persons: the FATHER, the SON and the HOLY SPIRIT. The Father corresponds to the chemical rays of sunlight; *No man hath seen God at any time.* The Son, who is the light of the world, corresponds to the light rays, the One whom we can see but not feel. The Holy Spirit corresponds to the heat rays, since He is felt in the lives of believers but is never seen. Thus John teaches us in the text that God is a TRINITY.

THE SOLAR SPECTRUM

When we analyze sunlight, we find that it consists of seven visible colors which compose the solar spectrum seen in the rainbow, or in the flashing colors of the well-cut diamond or beveled glass. If we pass a shaft of sunlight through a prism of glass, we find that the different colors have different angles of refraction, and when thrown upon a surface, the prism will appear in seven colors. At the upper end will be the violet and at the lower end will be the red. Above the violet we have ultraviolet rays, invisible to the human eye, as they are chemical rays. Below the red we have infrared rays, also invisible to the human eye. The fact that light can be divided into the seven basic colors from violet to red speaks of the perfection of the Godhead, for the number "seven" stands for perfection and God is perfect.

The spectrum speaks to us of the seven basic spheres of activity of the Godhead. The red speaks of His sacrifice; blue of His heavenly character; purple of His royal personality, and so on, throughout all the colors of the spectrum. God is perfect in all His attributes, graces and activities.

These seven colors of the spectrum are always found in sunlight.

OTHER CLASSIFICATIONS

We may again classify the rays which radiate forth from the sun in two groups.

1. Rays which are DEADLY to all living organisms.

2. Rays which are INDISPENSABLE and ESSENTIAL to living organisms.

Scientists teach that sunlight consists of several kinds of rays. If some of these rays should strike any organism which God has made, the result would be immediate death. But in this same sunlight are rays which are indispensable to the life of these organisms. These two kinds of rays are mixed in sunlight. If man is to continue to live on this earth, there must be a provision made by which the deadly rays can be diverted and the life-giving rays provided.

In creation, God made a provision for this very emergency. Encircling the earth is an envelope of gas which we call "air," extending upwards many, many miles in varying and decreasing density. This air has great refracting powers, so that when certain rays of light strike it, they are refracted and deflected. Death-dealing rays in sunlight have very high refracting properties so that when they strike this envelope of air they are sharply refracted with the result that most of them miss the earth and travel off, leaving a cone-shaped area of immunity. The life-giving rays, on the other hand, are not so easily refracted and pass through directly to the earth.

TWO BASIC ATTRIBUTES OF GOD

Speaking figuratively, we may say that God as light consists of two kinds of rays.

1. His "JUSTICE RAYS" which demand full payment for sin, infinite punishment for those who have transgressed His holy

law. These rays spell death, destruction and damnation for every creature in His sight because of sin.

2. His "LOVE RAYS" which yearn after the salvation, joy and redemption of His creation.

God is both these things. He is justice and He is love. If His justice were to strike it would mean our eternal destruction. A way must therefore be found by which His justice may be fully satisfied and filtered out and yet His love allowed to flow freely into the lives of His creatures.

THE SHIELD OF CHRIST

In the Lord Jesus Christ we have this provision fully made. Christ came into this world and partook of our human nature and on Calvary satisfied the just demands of God's law, fulfilled God's requirements and permitted the wrath of God in His judgment to be spent upon Himself. In other words, He refracted the "justice rays" of the God of light from the lives of those for whom He died. Christ becomes in redemption what the envelope of air around the earth is in nature. He is the Mediator interposed between God and man to avert God's wrath and bring us in contact with His perfect love. The sunlight, which without the interposition of the air would be our greatest enemy, becomes by its passage through the air our life-giver and benefactor. God, too, has become the justifier of those who believe. In Christ, God becomes our Life-Giver and Benefactor, the Saviour. *God is light, and in him is no darkness at all.*

RADIUM

One of the most concentrated forms of light with which man is familiar is in the radiation of the recently discovered element of radium, the most powerful light known to mankind. Radium light is composed almost entirely of actinic rays. It is not visible and cannot be felt and yet it is so powerful that an almost invisible particle of radium will emit enough chemical rays to cause certain death to anyone who comes in contact with it.

Again we find that radium sends forth two kinds of rays — rays that are DEADLY to living organisms and rays that are very BENEFICIAL to living organisms. If a group of individuals would gather within the confines of an ordinary room and place in their midst a particle of radium as big as the end of a lead pencil, there would not be time enough for any of these men to leave the room before the sentence of death would be written upon each one. So powerful are these rays that exposure to them spells certain death.

For several years, therefore, a search was made for an adequate shield that would filter out the deadly rays and yet admit the rays which were beneficial in the treatment of disease. Finally an element was found, and strikingly enough it was one of the most common elements found in the world. It was nothing else but LEAD. Lead is at the disposal of everyone — both rich and poor.

If we put this radium which is so deadly in its effect in capsules of metallic lead, we find that most of the death-dealing rays cannot pass freely through. We may now take the radium, which formerly caused death, and apply it to a cancer, or disease of the skin, or other part of the body, and find that the element which before would have killed the victim now does just the opposite. It kills the disease and gives life where before only death was possible.

The Lord also consists of these two rays — His JUSTICE and His eternal LOVE. In the Lord Jesus Christ we have the "capsule." God shining upon us through Him is changed from a consuming fire to a loving Father. Christ bore the shock, suffered God's wrath, satisfied His justice, and now He who could only condemn us because of our sin, through Christ becomes the death of our sin and the Author of our life. Instead of demanding death, He now diverts that which was causing our death and He becomes the Author of eternal life. *God is light, and in him is no darkness at all.*

It is worthy of note that the element which was found was lead. Both rich and poor may avail themselves of this element, which is at everyone's disposal. It was not gold nor platinum, which would be within the reach of only a few, but LEAD. So, too, Christ, through His sacrifice, made salvation available to all — poor and rich, small and great.

ILLUSTRATION

In closing we wish to leave with you an illustration that we believe will clinch this entire message. In the message entitled "The Chemistry of Calvary" we spoke about Moses presenting his atonement of typical blood to the Lord on Mount Sinai. Encouraged by the fact that his intercession had prevailed with the Lord and that He had accepted the solution of gold, Moses made a very bold and peculiar request. In Exodus 33:18-23 we read:

> And he said, I beseech thee, shew me thy glory.
> And he said, I will make all my goodness pass before thee, and I will proclaim the name of the Lord before thee; and will be gracious to whom I will be gracious, and will shew mercy on whom I will shew mercy.
> And he said, THOU CANST NOT SEE MY FACE: FOR THERE SHALL NO MAN SEE ME, AND LIVE.
> And the Lord said, Behold, there is a place by me, and thou shalt stand upon a rock:
> And it came to pass, while my glory passeth by, that I will put thee in a clift of the rock, and will cover thee with my hand while I pass by:
> And I will take away my hand, and thou shalt see my back parts: but my face shall not be seen.

This passage tells us of Moses' desire to see God's face. The Lord declares to him that this is impossible, but teaches Moses that only in Christ can we see God. The Lord places him upon a rock and the rock is cleft. Moses is hidden in the cloven rock and as God passes by he sees the Lord through the rock and lives.

In the twenty-third verse we have a rather awkward translation of a Hebrew word. We read that Moses saw "the Lord's back parts." The back part of an individual is that which follows after or comes behind, and has the significance here of the light which followed after, or the AFTERGLOW. It should read: *And I will take away my hand and thou shalt see my* AFTERGLOW: *but my face shall not be seen.*

THIS ROCK IS CHRIST

We know from I Corinthians 10 that this rock is Christ. Moses could not see God, but hidden in the "Rock of Ages" which is Christ, he saw God, and the rock filtered out the wrath of God and allowed only the "mercy rays" and the "love rays" of the Eternal to pass through. Today we know the truth of this in the light of the New Testament. We, too, cannot stand without a mediator before God, for *God is light, and in him is no darkness at all.* We need a shield between us and God. Of this the Psalmist spoke when he said: *The Lord God is a sun and shield.* God could never be our Sun unless He was also our Shield, as He is in the Person of the Lord Jesus Christ.

May I ask you who read this message — Are you hidden in the Rock, the "Rock of Ages," that was cleft for you? If not, may God grant you the realization that you can never stand in the presence of God without the Shield, the Rock, the Lord Jesus Christ.

> A wonderful Saviour is Jesus my Lord,
> A wonderful Saviour to me,
> He hideth my soul in the cleft of the rock,
> Where rivers of pleasure I see.
> He hideth my soul in the cleft of the rock
> That shadows a dry thirsty land;
> He hideth my life in the depths of His love,
> And covers me there with His hand.

Just a word in conclusion. The sinner will have to stand one day before the presence of this God who is the unapproachable Light. For a man to stand in the presence of God with sin upon him will be a worse experience than to be cast into hell itself. Darkness will be welcome to Christ-rejecting sinners. For this reason they will cry to the rocks and mountains to cover them from the face of Him who is the Light.

Dear reader, are you in Christ? Are you shielded by the Rock? If not, remember that Jesus said in John 5:24:

> Verily, verily, I say unto you, He that heareth my word, and believeth on him that sent me, hath everlasting life, and shall not come into condemnation; but is passed from death unto life.

CHAPTER 5

THE CHEMISTRY OF THE BOOK

"IN THE BEGINNING GOD" (Genesis 1:1).

This is the first verse of the first chapter of the first book of the Bible and constitutes the very foundation stone upon which all else that follows in the Book is built. Everything in the Bible stands or falls with this statement: IN THE BEGINNING GOD. Doubt this one simple opening statement of the Book, and you cannot and will not believe a single thing that follows in the rest of sacred Scripture. Infidelity begins right here, and faith rests itself here. It is probably the most important verse in the entire Scriptures. IN THE BEGINNING GOD — not "in the beginning a nebular mass" or "in the beginning a pool of warm slime" or "in the beginning some hairy monkeys swinging by their tails" but IN THE BEGINNING GOD.

If a man has any sense at all, he will believe this opening statement, and if he does not believe it, then according to this same God he is a "fool," for *the fool hath said in his heart, There is no God.* Here all faith must begin. Until you believe that *in the beginning God* you cannot believe in God's Son, the Lord Jesus Christ. *He that cometh to God must believe that* HE IS first of all. And once we believe this, all else becomes perfectly simple. For if I can believe that in the beginning there was nothing but God and that by Him everything was made that was made, then I can accept anything that God says about the things which He Himself has made.

Once upon a time there was no time. There was no creation. From a beginningless eternity, God was all alone in that perfect family-love life of Father, Son, and Holy Ghost. And there in that eternity He counseled with Himself and planned to make a creation and a universe. But He had NOTHING to begin with but Himself. And yet at the proper moment He spake and creation began. For *in the beginning God created the heaven and the earth.* When the time came He reached down the hand of His omnipotence into the great abyss of nothingness and threw it out into nowhere, and "nothing became SOMETHING" and from His Almighty fingers there stretched forth the universe with its planets and suns, its systems and constellations, as He sent them forth calling each one by their names while He hung them in the chandeliers of heaven and made them dance to the "music of the spheres." If I can believe this then I can believe that God could walk on the water, that He could make the sun and the moon obey His command and could lengthen Joshua's day. Then I can believe that He could part the Red Sea and make the Jordan stand on its feet. Then I can believe that He could turn water into blood and rain fire from heaven. Then I can believe that He could make an ass to speak, and rain bread from heaven for the children of Israel. It all depends on whether you believe that IN THE BEGINNING GOD.

This is the answer to all speculations and guesses. Compare with this the theorizing of man. Listen to man as he tells us that in the beginning there was a great superheated nebula and as it cooled it formed a semi-solid mass of matter. By its rapid revolutions, masses flew off from the mother mass and formed suns and worlds and other planets. Some cooled off and became inhabited. Others remained hot and became stars and suns. The one which we call "the earth" became covered with slime, and the slime began to crawl and finally developed fins and became a fish. The fish changed its fins for feet and became a reptile. The reptile grew hair and a tail and became a monkey, and the monkey caught his tail in a crotch of the tree, fell down to earth and suddenly awoke to find that he was your great-great-grandfather. That is the theory man would have us believe. But the Bible says: *God created man in his own image.* I ask you, what is the more reasonable explanation of the origin of this creation: this theory of man or the simple IN THE BEGINNING GOD CREATED?

IN THE BEGINNING GOD. The Bible contains no proof for the existence of God. You are expected to believe it. All evidence supports it. Even the heathen in darkest savagery believes in a god, whatever form that god may take. It remained for civilized man to invent the inane and insane theory of atheism. Even the inanimate creation extols and acknowledges its Creator.

> The heavens declare the glory of God; and the firmament sheweth his handywork.

The hills are said to skip like lambs at His approach, and all the trees of the field clap their hands in glee at the mention of His Name. Only man of all earth's creatures rebels against God and says in his heart, *There is no God.*

True science, therefore, can never be in conflict with the Bible. Wherever science and the Bible seem to conflict it is either because our scientific deductions are incorrect or our interpretation of Scripture is incorrect. Science, which comes from the word *scio,* meaning "to know," is not speculative or theoretical. True science deals with proved facts, and whereas today a great many things are called scientific, they are nothing of the kind. Any theory which is later proved to be false proves that it was unscientific. True science rests on unalterable and eternally established facts. Hence, when scientists have finally reached absolute truth, they will not be in conflict with the Bible, which itself is absolute truth.

Both science and theology suffer most from incapable amateur exponents. Sometimes science is correct and our interpretation of Scripture wrong, and then again all too often science is mere guesswork and appears only to contradict the Bible. True science never conflicts with the Bible, and true science has been the greatest handmaid of Scripture in supporting the claims of Holy Writ.

Let me give you an illustration or two. Up until the latter part of the nineteenth century, the skeptic and the higher critic took great pains to remind us that Moses could never have written the first five books of the Bible for the simple reason that scientists maintained that in the days when Moses was supposed to have lived there was no civilization at all. Man was still in the "Alley Oop stage" and was just emerging from the misty nebula of his slimy primal ancestors; said they, "In the day when Moses is supposed to have written these books there was no culture, no extensive social intercourse, no literature and no organized government or community life. Therefore Moses could not have written them." And this was the answer unbelief gave.

AN OLD WOMAN SCIENTIST

And then in 1877 something occurred which silenced these skeptics for all time. An old woman living in Egypt was digging in the ruins of an ancient city to obtain fertilizer for her little garden. In the ruins she dug up, she found what seemed to be bricks of clay, and she promptly ground them up and spread them on her garden, to return to her that fall in the form of onions and cucumbers and melons. How many of these bricks she ground up no one knows. But one day a missionary passing by, saw the bricks and suspected that they might have historical value and made the discovery known. As a result the archaeologists succeeded in buying the little plot of ground and dug up what little was left of an ancient library containing the correspondence between the Egyptians and the Babylonians in the days BEFORE MOSES. Only 350 of these tablets remained after the old lady's fertilizing experiment, but these 350 became of tremendous importance. Some are to be found today in the British Museum in London, some are in Berlin, and others are preserved in various other museums.

THE HITTITES

When the hieroglyphics were deciphered by the scientists, they found that these tablets were written in Moses' day and some before. In these records there was frequent mention made of the Hittites and the Amorites and the Canaanites who lived in Abraham's day. Some scientists had long been laughing at the mention of these nations in the Bible, asserting that they were purely fictitious names of nations that never existed. But God used the scientist's spade to prove otherwise.

THE HEBREWS

On some of these tablets they found the word HABIRI; and it is now known that the word means "HEBREWS." These particular tablets referred to southern Palestine and made mention, along with the Hittites and the other nations, of HABIRI or "HEBREWS" and we have the Biblical account of Abraham's pilgrimage to Palestine and his descendants, the Hebrews, dwelling there and conquering the land under Joshua.

These historic tablets are called the "Tel El Amarna," which was the name of the city where they were discovered by the little old woman. If you want a delightful time some afternoon or evening, go to the library, look up "Tel El Amarna" in an encyclopedia, and spend a couple of hours reading many of the things for which we do not have time now.

THE SCIENTIFIC BOOK

The Bible is the infallibly inspired revelation of God concerning Himself and His creation. Since He *made everything that was made,* He is the last and final authority on that which He made. Whether the Bible speaks of salvation, or astronomy, or psychology, or physiology, or anatomy, or geology, or history, or medicine, or surgery, or chemistry, or any other branch of science, it speaks with the same infallible authority.

How is it that Moses who was schooled for forty years in Egyptian philosophy and the sciences never incorporated any of the now discredited Egyptian supersititions in the books he wrote? In Moses' day people taught that a great man carried the earth on his shoulders and when the man sneezed there was an earthquake. But the Bible declared 3,500 years ago, *He hangeth the earth on nothing.* That was scientific. In Moses' day the practice of medicine, if it can be called that, was a mere mess and mass of superstition, boiling of toads' skins and demon incantations. Yet Moses, who was schooled in these superstitions, wrote the most scientific treatise on modern medicine, hygiene and sanitation the world has ever known. Today in our ultra-scientific age we have not added one thing or been able to improve on a single regulation Moses gave to the children of Israel concerning the handling of contagious diseases or the method of surgery.

PROPHYLAXIS

Today we know, since the discovery of bacteriology, that many diseases are caused by minute organisms called "bacteria" or "germs." In the prevention of disease we must isolate or quarantine those who are affected and spread these germs. So we isolate them in quarantine. But the Bible taught this 3,500 years ago. Israelites with leprosy or other communicable diseases were isolated outside the camp away from all others. When they had been healed they were declared clean by the priest, God's physician, and after thorough washing of the patient, all that he had touched was to be burned with fire or sterilized by fire. The saddle he rode on, the clothing he wore and the vessel he used and in some cases even the house were destroyed. Yes, Moses knew his bacteriology. We have known it only since the days of Pasteur and Koch and the microscope.

Have you ever watched a surgeon preparing for an operation? If you have, you noticed that he goes to the faucet, turns it on and then scrubs his hands for from ten to fifteen minutes UNDER THE TAP. Why does he not wash in a bowl? Because infection is carried to the body and hands by these germs which hide under the scales of the skin. The moment the physician, therefore, touches the water in the bowl the water becomes contaminated, and no matter how long he washes in that disease-laden water, his hands can never be rid of the germs. So he puts them under the tap and scrubs them, loosening the scales of skin tissue and the germs, which are carried away by the running water, till his hands are "surgically clean" and he can handle his patient without danger of infection. Moses knew all that 3,500 years before Pasteur was born. Read Leviticus 15 if you want an ultra-scientific discussion of the Biblical rules for disinfection of contagious disease. Read the thirteenth verse, which deals with the disinfection of the body of a man who had been infected:

> And when he that hath an issue is cleansed of his issue;
> then he shall number to himself seven days for his cleansing,

and wash his clothes, and bathe his flesh in running water, and shall be clean (Leviticus 15:13).

Why do we call attention to these things? Because we are living in a day and age when it is considered "smart" to doubt the Word of God. Those who still believe in the infallibility of the Bible are considered old-fashioned and odd. Our youth is taught that the Bible is only a book of religion and while there is much of value in it, it is not necessary to believe all of it. They hear it in the schools and even in the churches. I am not trying to defend the Bible. It needs no defence. It can stand on its own record. But I am bringing these messages in the hope that many of you, especially those of school and college age, may face the flood of atheistic teaching and propaganda in the firm conviction that we need never apologize for being old-fashioned enough to believe the whole Bible and that the real ignoramus is not the simple soul who dares to believe God but he is the fool who would accept the theories of man instead of the WORD of God. For *heaven and earth shall pass away, but my words shall not pass away*, said Jesus.

God has given us this Word and by this Word we shall be judged. You cannot be saved and not believe the Bible as the record of God to man. In I John 5:10 we read:

> He that believeth on the Son of God hath the witness in himself: he that believeth not God hath made him a liar; because he believeth not the RECORD that God gave of his Son.

Oh, sinner, believe Him today. God's Word is the truth and it tells us so plainly:

> He that believeth on him is not condemned: but he that believeth not is condemned already, because he hath not believed in the name of the only begotten Son of God (John 3:18).

II

MOSES THE SCIENTIST

> All scripture is given by inspiration of God, and is profitable for doctrine, for reproof, for correction, for instruction in righteousness (II Timothy 3:16).

For the prophecy came not in old time by the will of man: but holy men of God spake as they were moved by the Holy Ghost (II Peter 1:21).

The Bible is not only the Book of God which teaches man that he is lost and in need of salvation through faith in God's own Son, Jesus Christ, but it is at the same time the greatest Book on science which has ever been written. To deny this is to admit that you have never carefully studied the Bible. There is no other book in existence comparable to the Scriptures, in both its accuracy and scope of scientific information. No greater thing could be done to improve our American system of education than to introduce a compulsory course of Bible-study in our schools. Wholly apart from its spiritual content, the Bible contains more real literary value and truly scientific teaching than all other books taken together. It is the one Book which never needs revision and would be one course in our schools in which it would not be necessary for the parents to purchase a new edition of the textbook each year. The Bible needs no revision. Men have attempted it but with very poor success. The teachings Moses gave almost four thousand years ago are still as modern and up-to-date in every detail as they were when written and are ahead of the age in which we ourselves live. Can you imagine students in our schools being taught from other textbooks written over one thousand years ago? Imagine the medical student being taught the practice of medicine as it was one thousand years ago!

Moses was the greatest scientist who ever lived. On every subject which he treats he is an authority, and not one of his instructions given in the Pentateuch on medicine, surgery, hygiene, astronomy, psychology or other branches has ever needed correction or revision. And yet instead of the tried and proved truths of the Word of God, men would rather believe the vaporizings of man's hypothetical guesses that need to be changed with each new discovery than the simple record of the Word of God.

Instead of believing the simple and conclusive key to all knowledge given in the first verse of Scripture, *In the beginning God created,* man would rather believe the wholly unsupported, speculative and imaginative theory that we evolved from some ugly anthropoid ape, rather than the certain fact that we can trace our ancestry back to God Himself. How much more it adds to the dignity of man to be able to say, "God is my Father," than to have to admit that a hairy ape is the one to whom I owe my existence and my life.

How can intelligent men and women believe this silly "monkey business" when it is so much more reasonable and so much less embarrassing to trace our ancestry back to God Himself? There are folk who take great pride in their family and point out they have blue blood in their veins and that their great-great-grandfather fought in the Revolution; and then after priding themselves in some of these branches of their family tree they climb back a little farther until they find their great-great-great-great-grandfather either hanging by his neck or by the tail. As for me, I believe that *God created man in his own image, in the image of God created he him.*

True Science Always Agrees With the Bible

The Bible deals with every sphere of creation and touches fundamentally upon every scientific endeavor of man. It contains the foundation truths upon which all subsequent scientific knowledge is based. All scientific discovery is but an elaboration of that which is already fundamentally expressed in the Book. That sounds like a sweeping statement, and yet we shall substantiate that claim. Take first the matter of moral justice and our present system of jurisprudence. All these are based upon a document Moses received from the Lord almost four millenniums ago. I refer to the —

Ten Commandments

These ten words written first on tables of stone are still today the standard of justice. All our laws can be traced to these ten words. It was Moses who first laid down the right of fair trial for the individual by his establishment of the ten cities of refuge, which in reality were the courthouses of Israel. Here no accusation was received except upon the testimony of two or three witnesses. The much-praised democratic system of justice and fair trial was inaugurated by Moses. In addition to his great contribution in one field of law, we find that Moses also laid down the fundamental principles of agriculture and —

HORTICULTURE

We know today that selective breeding in cattle and careful pollinization of plants are the secret of the amazing development of better stock and magnificent fruits. Scientists have found out that breeding the select and the strong with the select and the strong produces a pure strain of superior stock, which in cows produces better beef and more milk, in sheep, more and better wool, in horses, bigger and stronger animals. In agriculture, we know that careful avoidance of cross-pollination and selective raising of a pure strain gives us better vegetables and fruits. The name of Burbank is synonymous with the application of this principle of selective and protective breeding. But Burbank, though he may have been an agnostic, simply discovered what Moses already taught three thousand years before Burbank was born. Listen to this:

> Thou shalt not sow thy vineyard with divers seeds: lest the fruit of thy seed which thou hast sown, and the fruit of thy vineyard, be defiled (Deut. 22:9).

Some of us have had to find out the truth of this by experience. If you plant citron and squash too near your watermelon, your melons will taste like citron. If you plant your field corn in the same patch with the sweet corn, your yellow bantam will taste like Number Two Hybrid. Only recently have men found the secret of producing better produce by avoiding cross pollination. Well, if they had read their Bibles they could have known before. Or turn to Leviticus 19:19:

> Thou shalt not let thy cattle gender with a diverse kind: thou shalt not sow thy field with mingled seed.

Besides a spiritual warning against intermingling with the Gentiles and the world, this has a scientific implication. It is God's instruction for the improvement of their stock by scientific selective breeding.

CONTROL OF PESTS

Besides all this, Moses gave instructions for the control of insect pests, which today are making farming an exceedingly difficult task. The farmer fights against the Colorado beetle, the Japanese beetle, the tomato worm, the corn borer, the rose bug, and a host of others. Most of these have a life cycle of one year. There are some that have a cycle which covers seven years and one at least seventeen years (the seventeen-year locust). After the eggs are laid, they enter the larval stage, in which they remain during the winter. When spring comes, the larvae emerge as full-grown insects, which repeat the cycle. These insects feed upon the same plants year after year.

Moses under inspiration commanded the children of Israel to set aside ONE YEAR IN SEVEN WHEN NO CROPS were to be raised. God promised to give sufficient harvest the sixth year to provide food for this period. Now see what this would do. Suppose it were the corn borer which, of course, did not trouble the farmers, for maize is a distinctly American plant. But it will serve as an illustration. The cornborer winters in the corn stalk, hatches in the spring and perpetuates itself by laying its eggs on the new ears of corn. Now, if one year in seven NO CORN AT ALL IS RAISED there is nothing for the borer to subsist upon and the pest is controlled by this simple expedient. Today we have a weak copy of this system in the rotating of crops, but at best it does not approach the success of the Sabbatic year. Then there was the Year of Jubilee after every seven Sabbatic years, which would serve to eliminate the insects which had a cycle of seven years or more or less and which were not affected by the one year in seven.

INDUSTRY AND MORALS

Space will not permit us to go into all the ramifications of the Bible laws, which affected every realm of human endeavor, but we must mention one more which occurs in this same verse in Leviticus 19:19. It deals with the tailoring profession:

> Thou shalt not sow thy field with mingled seed: neither shall a garment mingled of linen and woolen come upon thee.

The Israelite was permitted to wear linen or wool but they were not to be mixed in the same garment. The logic of this is known to all who know anything about cloth. Linen and wool have different degrees of shrinkage. The degree of shrinkage varies in these two articles so that for best wear and lasting form the two were not to be mingled. Mixed fabrics are soon filled with folds and creases due to this inequality of shrinkage, and thus the garment tends to wear out in the uneven places. We have incorporated this very principle into a commercial proverb. When we want to state that an article is of the very best we say, "It is all wool and a yard wide."

WOMEN'S DRESS

The Bible also teaches that the matter of dress has a moral application. I am going to give you a verse that will be unpopular with many of you, but I am not aiming at being popular with you; I have one desire: that I may be popular with Him who sent me to preach the Gospel. This verse pertains to the dress of men and women. You will find it in Deuteronomy 22:5:

> The woman shall not wear that which pertaineth unto a man, neither shall a man put on a woman's garment: for all that do so are abomination unto the Lord thy God.

God emphatically declares that He wants the distinction of the sexes sacredly maintained. Man was created for a different purpose than the woman, and the woman has a unique function separate from the man. It is the decree of God that man should be the toiler and the woman the home-builder. God commanded the man, *In the sweat of thy face shalt thou eat bread.* Anything which draws the woman away from the home and breaks down the unique separate position of the woman and motherhood is an abomination of the Lord. To safeguard the dignity of womanhood and to emphasize her entirely separate function, God gave this injunction against women wearing men's clothes. And whenever this fundamental law is violated that nation decays morally and spiritually. No nation can continue in the blessing of the Lord which permits the breakdown of the distinction between the sexes. The current custom of women's dress is a greater menace to the welfare of American than invasion from a foreign power. It is an evil within our gates and I call upon all Christian women to be faithful to God and to "rather be a horse and buggy than stoop to the vile and pagan practice of modern woman's dress."

May I speak plainly? God meant that a woman's body and the man's, too, should be covered. God made the first garments for man and they are specifically called "coats," a word which signifies that they covered the body from the shoulders down, to remind us that the upper part of the body should be covered as well as the rest. The modern dress of our women on the beaches, the streets and even in our business places is an invitation to moral decay, social collapse and the judgment of the Lord. Shorts, my friend, are still nothing else than undergarments, and beach pajamas should only be worn on the street if you intend to sleep there. This applies to men as well. To see men, even preachers, running about in public with only a pair of shorts is a disgrace to civilization, a return to the jungle and an abomination to the Lord. And except on those occasions where the emergency of special work demands it, the woman, according to Scripture, is never to be seen in man's dress no matter how stylish and "natty" the derby and the breeches may look on "milady."

OLD-FASHIONED?

I hear some one say, "That is all Old Testament and law. We are living in the new dispensation of grace." Listen to Paul in the New Testament:

> I will therefore that the younger women marry, bear children, guide the house, give none occasion to the adversary to speak reproachfully (I Timothy 5:14).

The woman's place is in the home and there is nothing more Godlike than MOTHERHOOD. The breakup of the home and the refusal of the blessings of parenthood are the curse of modern civilization.

In regard to dress Paul also has something to say. In I Timothey 2:9 we read:

> In like manner also, that women adorn themselves (God wants you to adorn your bodies as the temples of the Holy Ghost. There is no injunction against dressing beautifully and neatly) in MODEST APPAREL.

Or listen to Peter as he speaks of women adorning themselves.

> But let it be the hidden man of the heart, in that which is not corruptible, even the ornament of a meek and quiet spirit, which in the sight of God is of great price (I Peter 3:4).

Oh, Christian men and women, "DARE TO BE DIFFERENT." I do not mean that you must wear "peculiar dress" but rather that, while you dress neatly and beautifully, you do it modestly because of Him who, when you were naked through sin, clothed you from head to foot with the garments of salvation and His own precious righteousness.

Oh, sinner, you are still naked before God. And God will not permit anyone to come to Him naked through sin. You must be clothed, and the Lord Jesus Christ has provided for you a garment which you may have by faith, a garment which will fit you to stand in His presence without shame and contempt. May God help you to accept His provision by faith today.

III

> Search the scriptures; for in them ye think ye have eternal life: and they are they which testify of me. Do not think that I will accuse you to the Father: there is one that accuseth you, even Moses, in whom ye trust.
> For had ye believed Moses, ye would have believed me: for he wrote of me.
> But if ye believe not his writings, how shall ye believe my words? (John 5:39, 45, 46, 47).

These words of the Lord Jesus Christ to the Jews of His day bring us face to face with the issue of believing this Bible as the eternally infallible revelation of God or rejecting it as something less than an absolute and infallible authority. Jesus says, "If you do not believe the writings of Moses, how can you believe MY WORDS?"

The Bible is a unit. We speak of the sixty-six books of the Bible, but in reality they are but chapters of the ONE BOOK, the HOLY SCRIPTURES. Though written by some forty different authors, over a period of some eighteen centuries, in at least eight different countries, by men who range from peasants to kings, and uncouth fishermen to educated scholars, yet all have but one message, and none ever contradicts the other. These forty writers wrote in their homeland and in exile, in palace and in prison, in days of brightest prosperity and deepest gloom, in days of victory and times of captivity, and yet all of them have but one theme and all harmonize to the minutest detail.

Now this would be absolutely impossible without admitting the supernatural in the writing of the Bible. It is simply unimaginable that we could, today, gather sixty-six books, written in eight different countries, by forty authors, each with his own particular viewpoint, which would harmonize perfectly and be entirely free from contradictions. It is simply unimaginable. Yet the Bible is such a Book. For, whereas the Bible had forty HUMAN authors, it had but *One* DIVINE author. The same Holy Spirit who inspired Moses to write the first five books of the Bible with its perfect revelation is the same unchangeable Holy Spirit who also moved upon the Apostle John on the Isle of Patmos to write the closing book of the canon of Scripture almost two thousand years after Moses wrote his works.

There is no salvation for those who deny the super-natural inspiration of the whole Bible. To reject part is to reject all. You cannot believe on the Lord Jesus Christ and doubt the writings of Moses, for Jesus said, in the passage at the head of this section:

> For had ye believed Moses, ye would have believed me: for he wrote of me.
> But if ye believe not his writings, how shall ye believe MY WORDS?

MOSES THE ASTRONOMER

We have pointed out that Moses was the greatest scientist who ever lived. All his revelations still stand today because He received His knowledge of science DIRECT from God who is the Creator of all matter with which science deals. Moses was not only a specialist in one branch of science but in every branch, whether it be medicine, hygiene, surgery, astronomy, physics, psychology or geology. Probably one of the oldest of all sciences is that of astronomy. The ancients in the Orient, because of the splendid opportunities afforded by the clear night skies, seem first to have directed their attention to the heavens and the study of the heavenly bodies. However, until the discovery of the telescope, their knowledge of the heavens was very limited. Until the discovery of the polarascope and other modern laboratory instruments, but little was known of the science of the spheres. But Moses knew all about it. The Bible teaches that the earth is round says about God that He *sitteth upon the circle* [*globe*] *of the earth.* Solomon already knew the science of evaporation and rainfall, and anticipated modern meteorology by saying:

> All the rivers run into the sea; yet the sea is not full; unto the place from whence the rivers come, thither they return again (Ecclesiastes 1:7).

JOSHUA'S LONG DAY

The skeptics have had great sport with the so-called "mistake of Joshua's long day." They have pointed out that the writer of the book of Joshua was very deficient in his knowledge of astronomy. The record in Joshua 10:12, tells us that Joshua said:

> Sun, stand thou still upon Gibeon; and thou, Moon, in the valley of Ajalon.

The critics tell us sneeringly that if Joshua had known what he was talking about he would not have commanded the sun to stand still, but the earth. We know that the sun does not revolve around the earth but that the day and the night are produced by the revolution of the earth upon its own axis and the year is formed by the revolution of the earth around the sun. Hence, to lengthen the day it would be necessary to slow up the revolution of the earth, and so Joshua's command to the sun was misdirected. It should have been spoken to the earth instead. It has now been definitely established by scientists that the earth has two movements: one around the sun, once in a little more than 365 days, making our solar year; the earth also spins upon its own axis once in about twenty-four hours, causing our day.

GRAVITATION OF THE SUN

Furthermore, is an established fact that this spinning of the earth which causes the day, is the result of the gravitation of the sun. That is, the sun exerts a strong pull upon the earth and because the earth is inclined upon its axis this pull causes the earth to rotate and whirl around. The cause of the earth's spin is the activity of the sun with its pull upon the earth's mass. Therefore, to stop the earth from turning it would be necessary to stop the "pull" of the sun. A reduction in the gravitational pull of the sun would result in a slowing down of the rotation of the earth.

"DAMAM"

Joshua knew all this 3,500 years ago, although we have but recently discovered it. Therefore he did not make the mistake of telling the earth to stand still, but, instead, he commanded the sun to do so. The expression "STAND STILL" in Joshua 10 is DAMAM in the Hebrew. It means "STOP WORKING" — "CEASE ACTING." When anything stops working it stands still, of course, and so the translators have rendered the word DAMAM "STAND STILL." Joshua commanded the sun to STOP its gravitation, to stop its pull, and when that happened, the earth began to slow up and the day was lengthened according to the infallible record in the Book. Discoveries of scientists once more demonstrate that any theory which contradicts the record of Scripture is WRONG always.

SURGERY

Leaving the field of astronomy, look for a moment at the knowledge of the Bible writers in the matter of surgery. Here we have sill another example of the infallibility of the books of Moses. The children of Israel were led out of Egypt under the direction of the great lawgiver. Soon after they left the land, God began to give them through Moses a complete digest of laws and regulations to guide them in every realm of their national, social, religious and domestic existence. Among these regulations He gave the command that all male children in the camp of Israel were to be circumcised. This we know today is one of the most modern hygienic measures in the prevention of disease. We have found that circumcision is probably the greatest factor in the prevention of venereal disease. So merely from the standpoint of hygiene this command was up-to-date and modern.

But the Lord commanded not only circumcision of all males but He gave strict instructions concerning the EXACT TIME when this minor surgical operation was to be performed. It was to be done in every case on the EIGHTH DAY — not on the seventh nor on the ninth but on the *eighth* day. Ask your physician if he knows the scientific reason for this.

INFECTION AND HEMORRHAGE

Only recently have scientists discovered the reason for this. With our modern laboratory equipment, we have been able to analyze the blood of the newborn infant. In this blood, in addition to the plasma, the red cells, and the white cells, and blood platelets, scientists have discovered many interesting chemical elements. This blood contains the "antibodies" which are the disease-resisting elements in the blood. Were it not for these antibodies in the blood all of us would succumb very shortly to infection. But these chemical antibodies counteract the infection and the toxins and thus prevent disease. In many cases we introduce these antitoxins into the system to augment those which are there or supply them when they are lacking. Hence we have vaccines, serums, antitoxins and toxin antitoxins.

In the newborn babe, the blood is saturated with these antitoxins or disease-fighting elements which are received from the mother before birth. For the first week of life, therefore, the child is protected against infection, and, indeed, infections (except of the eyes) are rare in the newborn infant.

But there is a second element in the infant's blood which

we shall call the "blood clotting ability," to avoid more technical and scientific terms. In the blood there are elements which coagulate when a vein or artery is severed. These elements called *fibrinogen* and *thrombinogen* function to form a stringy network much like a spider's web when a wound is produced. This fine network forms a mesh in which the solid elements of the blood (the corpuscles) become ensnared and form a firm clot which plugs the severed vein or artery and thus stops the bleeding. This we call "blood clotting."

In the newborn babe the elements needed for rapid clotting are present in a very insufficient amount. Wounds, therefore, would be very serious because of the danger of hemorrhage, caused by this deficiency in clotting material. But these elements increase rapidly in the blood until they reach their normal concentration at about the beginning of the second week of life.

Now follow carefully. Since the disease-fighting content of the blood, the antibodies, begin to decrease after the first week, operations AFTER that time are attended with the danger of infection. But since the coagulating properties of the infant's blood (the clotting ability) do not reach their normal number until the end of the first week, operations BEFORE that time are attended with the danger of HEMORRHAGE. Hence the safest time for the surgery of circumcision is at that very point where both the disease-fighting qualities and the blood clotting ability are at their highest point. Did Moses know surgery? Where did he get his information?

Scientists recognize these facts today. A prominent physician and surgeon in the city of Detroit some time ago informed me that in the leading hospitals in Detroit, doctors are not permitted to circumcise infants until after the FIRST week. They have finally found out what Moses knew almost four thousand years ago. Ah, friend, can you still doubt this Living Word of God? Did Moses know surgery as well as astronomy, and hygiene, and medicine and chemistry? Living in an age that was choked with superstitions, he gave these revelations millenniums ahead of modern scientific discovery.

This will explain why, of all the countless millions of Hebrew children which have been circumcised since God first told Abraham to perform the operation on his family, there has been so little complication by infection and hemorrhage. Think of the crude methods used in days past by crude and often filthy rabbis; and yet, generally speaking, complications have been rare.

SPIRITUAL LESSON

But the rite of circumcision had a deeper meaning as well. Whatever your church's interpretation may be of this rite, one thing is certain: It was the mark of separation of God's people. It was a national and a family mark. It taught them they were not of the world but were a peculiar people. And it has its application to the Christian today. Paul writes in Philippians 3:3:

> For we are the circumcision, which worship God in the spirit, and rejoice in Christ Jesus, and have no confidence in the flesh.

Circumcision in the spiritual sense is also a hygienic measure. It represents the "cutting away of the filth of the flesh." You can never be free from the defilement of the world and the infection of besetting sin until you too by the scalpel of the Word have cut away the things of the flesh and the world. The Church today is infected with worldliness and sin, and anemic from spiritual hemorrhage because we have not been willing to let God operate on us and cut away the things of self, the world and the flesh.

Oh, Christian, are you defeated and weak? Do you miss the joy and the victory in your Christian life? Then examine yourself and see what it is of the flesh that infects your spiritual life and drains you of the power of the Spirit of God. Examine your heart today and yield everything to Him. It may hurt and smart and bleed, but, oh, it will make you clean and pure and happy in Him.

And, sinner, what is there in all this for you? Simply this: The Word of God is SURE. You cannot be saved without BE-LIEVING GOD'S WORD. In this message I have not tried to defend the Word. It needs no defence by me. But I have tried to show you that you can SAFELY TRUST GOD. You need not be afraid to rest your whole destiny on THIS WORD which is the IMMU-

TABLE promse of God. Oh, believe the RECORD of the Word. John says in his First Epistle:

> He that believeth on the Son of God hath the witness in himself: he that believeth not God hath made him a liar; because he believeth not the RECORD that God gave of his Son.

I have tried to show you that this WORD of God is TRUST-WORTHY, whether spoken by Moses, or Jesus, or David, or John. Oh, TRUST HIS WORD TODAY.

CHAPTER 6

THE CHEMISTRY OF PRAYER

LORD, TEACH US TO PRAY

And it came to pass, that, as he was praying in a certain place, when he ceased, one of his disciples said unto him, LORD, TEACH US TO PRAY (Luke 11:1).

LORD, TEACH US TO PRAY. The disciples of Jesus did not ask the Lord, "Teach us to preach" or "Teach us to sing," but they asked for this one great thing; *Lord, teach us to pray.* I would a hundred times rather be a great "prayer" than a great preacher. I would far rather have the power of prayer to move the very powers of heaven than to have the power of preaching to move the masses of men on earth. Men can train other men to become great preachers and orators but only Jesus can teach men and women to become great masters of the art and the science of prayer. More is accomplished by prayer than has ever been or will be accomplished by all the preaching in the world, for without prayer even our preaching becomes powerless and empty.

Prayer is everybody's gift and privilege. Whereas we often need preparation and training to become efficient preachers and personal workers, the gift of prayer is offered to all, and all may become the wielders of the very powers of Omnipotence. Not all men are called to be pastors or preachers or teachers or evangelists or exhorters. God gives to every man his gift and his task, according to his ability. But no such restrictions are placed upon the art of prayer. This gift is for all. Jesus says, *Men ought always to pray, and not to faint.* One needs no special call to the ministry of prayer as one needs a call to the work of evangelism or the pastorate. If you are called to preach, God will make you preach, and if you cannot preach, just make up your mind that you have never been called to this ministry. But no limitations are set on prayer. The humblest and most ignorant child of God may have as much power in prayer as the greatest and most learned professor. It is the privilege of all.

Nevertheless, the fact remains that the power of prayer is the power which is least exercised by the average believer. Many are sighing because they cannot do great things for the Lord, and forget that there is no power committed to the believer greater than the power of prayer and intercession. God needs more "prayers" far more than more preachers. No Christian grace is more neglected than the privilege of prayer, and the sad condition of carnality and worldliness, with loss of power and indifference among believers, can be traced to the lack of intelligent, trusting prayer on the part of the Christian Church. And so the cry of our hearts must be again the cry of the disciple of Jesus when he said, *Lord, teach us to pray*. Yes, "Lord, teach ME to pray."

THE PATTERN OF PRAYER

In answer to the question of the disciple, the Lord Jesus gave a definite answer. In the corresponding passage in Matthew, Jesus lays down some general rules concerning prayer and then follows it with a Model Prayer usually called the "Lord's Prayer" but which was in reality the "Disciples' Prayer." The Lord's Prayer is found in the seventeenth chapter of John, in the great High Priestly Prayer of our Lord just before He went to Calvary. But for the present we shall use the accepted term "Lord's Prayer" for that familiar prayer which Jesus taught His disciples. But before studying this Model Prayer and pattern for all prayer we must note some things Jesus said just before He gave the disciples this Model Prayer. Let us turn to Matthew 6:5-8.

> And when thou prayest, thou shalt not be as the hypocrites are: for they love to pray standing in the synagogues and in the corners of the streets, that they may be seen of men. Verily I say unto you, They have their reward.

But thou, when thou prayest, enter into thy closet, and when thou hast shut the door, pray to thy Father which is in secret: and thy Father which seeth in secret shall reward thee openly.

But when ye pray, use not vain repetitions as the heathen do: for they think that they shall be heard for their much speaking.

Be ye not therefore like unto them: for your Father knoweth what things ye have need of, before ye ask him.

Then follows the familiar so-called Lord's Prayer. But notice that in the words I have just read the Lord presents the negative teaching on prayer and in the Lord's Prayer He gives us the POSITIVE teaching on prayer. In the verses Matthew 6:5-8 He warns us concerning things we must NOT DO when we pray, and in verses 9-13 he tells us WHAT TO pray and How to pray.

Prayer is a science. Prayer means study. However, although we study to become preachers and Sunday school teachers and personal workers, very few of us make a study of the art of prayer and the science of prayer as taught in the Bible. In our Bible schools and seminaries we have many departments for the teaching of various subjects, such as Church History, Greek, Hebrew, homiletics, Bible synthesis, Bible doctrine, etc., but where is the department that teaches the "SCIENCE of prevailing prayer"? Oh, there are prayer meetings, thank God, where we can PRACTICE prayer, and would to God there were more of them, but the subject of prayer is important enough to merit a separate course taught by men who themselves have been taught of God.

As we hear men pray, and when we study our own prayer life, what a sorry spectacle presents itself. How little thought we give to making our prayers Scriptural and intelligent! How little we follow the rules of our Lord Jesus as laid down in the passage we have just read! How long our public prayers are, and how few and short our private closet prayers! How much of vain repetition! How much of the marks of the hypocrites in our prayers and how often we pray for things which God's wisdom forbids Him to answer.

The Negative Teaching On Prayer

In Matthew 6:5-18 the Lord Jesus tells us some things we should Not do when we pray. Listen to Him again:

> And when thou prayest, thou shalt not be as the hypocrites are.

"Don't pray like a hypocrite," He says to His disciples. Now what are the characteristics of a hypocrite's prayer, according to the Lord Jesus?

First, a hypocrite's prayer is Public. Notice that they love to pray in the synagogues and on the corners of the streets. They pray to be seen and heard of men. To make themselves more prominent and sure of notice by other men, they stand up, whereas they should be on their faces in the dust. The Pharisee in the Temple Stood and prayed thus, whereas the poor publican durst not lift his head toward heaven but smote his breast and cried, *God be merciful to me a sinner.* Hypocrites are great prayers. They spend much time in so-called "prayer" but the sad thing is that it is always public and never private. Turn to the words of Jesus as found in Matthew 23:14:

> Woe unto you, scribes and Pharisees, hypocrites! for ye devour widows' houses, and for a pretence make Long Prayer: therefore ye shall receive the greater damnation.

It is a pretty safe rule that "the longer a man prays in public, the less he has prayed in private." Any child of God who has prayed earnestly in private will be able to complete his public prayer quickly. Study the prayers of Scripture and see how many long public prayers you can find. Study the prayers of the Lord Jesus and you will discover two things:

First, that He was a man of great prayer. He spent whole nights on the mountain without sleep, praying to God. But can you find a long prayer in His public ministry? The Model Prayer of our Lord was so brief that you can pray it reverently in about thirty seconds. This is to my knowledge the longest public prayer the Lord Jesus ever offered. The next longest is recorded in John 17. It is His High Priestly Prayer in the upper room with His disciples. The prayer as recorded by John would consume about two and a half minutes. Let me repeat, "Long prayers in public are often an indication of very little prayer in private." Let us heed the words of our blessed Lord in Matthew 6:

> But thou, when thou prayest, enter into thy closet, and when thou hast shut thy door, pray to thy Father which is in secret.

When we pray, we pray to God, and not that men may hear us. The world does not care to hear you pray. You are commanded to preach to them, not to pray to them.

VAIN REPETITION

The Lord also gives us another warning. This is in regard to vain repetitions. Read again Matthew 6:7:

> But when ye pray, use not vain repetitions as the heathen do: for they think that they shall be heard for their much speaking.

Vain repetitions! How we need to emphasize those words. *Vain repetitions!* How guilty many of us are of this error. How stereotyped our prayers become! How we use the same hackneyed phrases over and over again! I trust you will bear with me as I say this, for I mean it seriously. Many prayers consist of the wearying repetition of the phrases "Our Father," "Holy Father" and "Lord Jesus." This is the substance of many prayers: "Our Father which art in heaven, we come to Thee, our Father, and ask Thee, O Father, to bless us this day, O Heavenly Father. Heavenly Father, we have sinned, and we pray, Heavenly Father, that Thou wilt forgive us, Father, for all we have done, Heavenly Father." And so on. I do hope you will forgive me if I have seemed irreverent, but I desire to warn against this type of prayer which is so dangerously prevalent today. Take out the vain repetitions and the prayer would be half as long. Jesus warns against this use of vain repetitions and gives us an example in the Model Prayer, in which these repetitions are never used.

THE REASON

We use these vain repetitions because we have never made

a study of Scriptural prayer. Our petition is a haphazard affair. There are certain definite rules of prayer which, if we will heed them, will teach us the Scriptural science of prevailing prayer. Study your prayer life. Examine your prayers. Compare them with the prayers of Jesus and of Paul. Purpose in your heart to become a great "prayer."

II

THE ELEMENTS OF PRAYER

After this manner therefore pray ye: Our Father which art in heaven, Hallowed be thy name.

Thy kingdom come. Thy will be done in earth, as it is in heaven.

Give us this day our daily bread.

And forgive us our debts, as we forgive our debtors.

And lead us not into temptation, but deliver us from evil: for thine is the kingdom, and the power, and the glory, for ever. Amen (Matt. 6:9-13).

Jesus said, in introducing this prayer, *After this manner therefore pray ye.* He did not say, "Whenever you pray, repeat these words or read them from a prayer book, and in meaningless parrotlike repetition chant this prayer at every one of your services until the congregation can do it without even waking from the sweet slumber into which the somniferous sermon of the monotoned preacher has cradled them." That is to be guilty of the very error against which the Lord Jesus warned His disciples when He said:

But when ye pray, use not vain repetitions.

Rather, the Lord Jesus said, AFTER THIS MANNER PRAY YE. This prayer is a model, not in the sense that it is to be vainly repeated, but the structure of this prayer should be the model for your prayers. We will not discuss here the dispensational character of the prayer. As you probably know, this prayer has its primary application to Israel and will undoubtedly be prayed in the time of Jacob's trouble. It is a kingdom prayer. We are interested primarily in the fact that Jesus said, "AFTER THIS MANNER THEREFORE PRAY YE." Let this prayer be the pattern for your praying. Notice that it is a very brief prayer. Then too it is a specific prayer which covers in thirty seconds the whole scope of our needs for spirit, soul and body. Notice again there is no vain repetition; this prayer is definite and to the point.

LORD, TEACH US HOW TO PRAY LIKE THAT!

THREE ELEMENTS OF PRAYER

A study of this brief prayer of the Lord Jesus will reveal that it easily divides itself into three "LOOKS." There is first an "UP-LOOK" then an "INLOOK" and finally an "OUTLOOK." The first element of prayer looks to God: *Our Father which art in heaven, Hallowed be* THY NAME. THY *kingdom come.* THY *will be done in earth as it is in heaven.* Then comes the part that looks to self and its needs: "Give us this day our daily bread." Then comes the "OUTLOOK" to others around us: *Forgive us our debts, as we forgive our debtors.* These three elements of complete prayer have been called —

1. COMMUNION
2. PETITION
3. INTERCESSION

COMMUNION is that phase of prayer in which we turn our attenion toward GOD. It is the first essential element and the one on which the others are based. The second element is PETITION, in which our attention is turned inward upon our own needs; and then we turn our attention OUTWARD, and in INTERCESSION our interest in prayer loses every element of SELFISHNESS and we become concerned about the needs of those round about us.

COMMUNION

Until the soul is established in communion of prayer there can be no answer to our petitions and no power in our intercession. Communion is that part of prayer which removes every hindrance between God and ourselves. It is that act of worship and adoration which seeks only the glory of God and subordinates all our personal petitions to His will and to His glory. It is the attitude of complete submission. It seeks nothing for self, but is only occupied with HIM and His goodness and His loveliness. Communion establishes the CONTACT so that our petitions can reach Him and our intercessions for others can be heard and answered by God. COMMUNION is the line that connects our soul with the battery of God's power. When this line is down our petitions are but idle chatter. Here is the great dynamo of the omnipotence of God. We are poor, needy creatures. A line must be strung from God's heart to ours before the power can flow into our lives. This we call worship. It is the first duty of man.

Take an example from the order of the first five books of the Bible, usually called the "Pentateuch." In Genesis we read of man's sin and ruin. In Exodus we see God's redemption by blood. Then follows Leviticus with its ritual for the worship of the children of Israel. It is the GREAT WORSHIP BOOK of the Old Testament. Then follows Numbers, the book of ISRAEL'S WALK from Egypt to Canaan. And then follows Deuteronomy, the BOOK OF THE LAW, or the BOOK OF WORKS.

This is ever God's order. After man is redeemed he must first learn to WORSHIP before he will ever be able to WALK as he should, and not until he has learned to WORSHIP and to WALK will his WORK amount to anything. How many young Christians need to learn this lesson! They want to go to work immediately and to preach and teach and Do things for God. All this is fine but it amounts to nothing until they have learned first of all the indispensable need of WORSHIP — the need to be quiet and sit at His feet and worship Him.

MARY AND MARTHA

Consider the story of Mary and Martha. When the Lord Jesus was being entertained by these two lovely sisters, fretful, working, toiling Martha complained because Mary did nothing but sit at Jesus' feet. She asked Jesus to rebuke her sister and command Mary to lend a hand. But Jesus answered, *Martha, Martha, thou art careful and troubled about many things: but one thing is needful: and Mary hath chosen that good part.* What did the Lord mean? Did He rebuke Martha's faithful service? No, not at all. He rebuked her because her service had not been preceded by WORSHIP. Her service would have been much better if she, like Mary, had taken time to sit at Jesus' feet. Later Martha again served, but Jesus did not rebuke her at all. Evidently she had learned the lesson and taken time to WORSHIP FIRST.

Notice, then, that communion is the first element in the Lord's Prayer: "OUR FATHER *which art in heaven, Hallowed be* THY *name.*" Most of our prayers are all "petition" and asking for things. Do you ever go to Him when you do not want a single thing? Do you ever go to Him to admire Him and thank Him for what He *is*, and not only for what He has done for you? Do you ever go to Him just to tell Him how precious He is, and how you admire Him just FOR WHAT HE IS, and not only for what HE IS TO YOU?

I like to have my boys come to me just to tell me how much they think of their "dad." When one of them comes to me and puts his arms around my neck and says, "Dad, you are the greatest dad anybody ever had," I become suspicious that they have something they are leading up to and I ask, "Well, what do you want?" And then when he says, "Nothing, Dad, I just wanted to be near you and tell you how much I thank God for you," my heart swells with joy. Do you ever do that with HIM? To do it there must be nothing between. In true communion, everything between you and the Lord is right, the lines are up, you are connected with Central and the power can flow through. When this connection is gone, your prayers cannot be heard.

Communion, the first element in prayer, DOES SOMETHING To Us, whereas in petition we have something done FOR us, and by intercession we have something done THROUGH us. But before something can be done FOR us or THROUGH US, something must be done TO Us. And this we get in COMMUNION. If we keep the lines clear and allow nothing to come between us and the Lord, then when a crisis comes and we need something quickly, we can just turn on the switch of PETITION and get what we will. But if the line of communion is DOWN and the test comes, we have no power and our prayers are not heard for we have to stop and string up the line and make the connection by confession, and by that time it may be too late for help. Keep the line open and then suddenly in sickness, temptation, trial, or even in the shadow of death, you can turn to Him and get what you need. COMMUNION STRINGS THE LINE. Petition THROWS THE SWITCH and INTERCESSION CONNECTS OTHERS WITH your machinery of prayer and power.

Before we need something done FOR *us* we need something done To us. That is our great need. Is there anything that has broken the connection, my friend? It should never be. This is the element of prayer that is referred to in the words, *Men ought always to pray and not to faint,* and in Paul's words, *Pray without ceasing.* Certainly this does not mean that we must unceasingly mumble words of prayer. It refers rather to this constant communion with God which keeps the lines open for every emergency. That is what Jesus taught when He said:

> If ye abide in me, and my words abide in you, ye shall ask what ye will, and IT SHALL BE DONE [notice DONE and not GIVEN] unto you.

Before we ask God to give us anything in prayer we need something DONE To Us and IN Us, and then our prayers will be answered. If I regard iniquity in my heart the Lord will not hear me.

Oh, friend, the important question is not "What does prayer GET for you?" but "What does prayer Do for you?" After Jesus had prayed, the disciples saw something in Him that made them cry out, LORD, TEACH US TO PRAY.

PETITION

The second element in prayer is called PETITION. Whereas communion looks to God, in petition the face is turned to the needs of self. In our Lord's Model Prayer He covers all material and spiritual need in the words:

> Give us this day our daily bread.
> And forgive us our debts, as we forgive our debtors.
> And lead us not into temptation, but deliver us from evil.

If the FIRST element of communion has been faithfully observed, and we have sat at His feet and learned how HE prayed, then PETITION becomes a very simple thing. Then we have but to ask anything according to His will and God will give it. When our petitions fail it is because the line is down and the connection is broken. There are many, many reasons given in the Bible for unanswered prayers. We have time to mention but a few.

First of all, if there is unconfessed known sin in our lives the Lord will not hear us. This does not mean that we are sinless, for if we were there would be little need of prayer. But when we come to Him there must be an honest confession of sin for *If I regard iniquity in my heart, the Lord will not hear me.*

In Matthew 18 and Luke 17 the Lord Jesus tells us that an unforgiving spirit against a brother will hinder our prayers from being answered. *Therefore if thou bring thy gift to the altar, and there rememberest that thy brother hath ought against thee; leave there thy gift before the altar, and go thy way; first be reconciled to thy brother, and then come and offer thy gift* (Matthew 5:23-24). Maybe some of you will find here the reason why God seems not to have heard your cry.

Furthermore, the Lord expects us to answer some of our own prayers. We have no right to ask God to do something for us that we are able to do ourselves. It is a useless waste of time to ask God to save sinners if you do not contact those sinners and tell them the story of the Gospel. I remember one man in a church I served who prayed each Sunday very fervently, "Oh, Lord, save the sinners in the audience," but he had never tried to invite one sinner to come into the audience. The farmer may pray the Lord to give him a good crop of corn, but if he does not plant corn he will not have a crop. God does not do things that way. You may pray all you want to for the heathen to be saved through the preaching of the missionaries but if you hold back your money from these missionaries your prayer is merely idle "cant." You may pray all day long for God to bless the radio ministry in the awakening of Christians and salvation of souls but if you do not support it when you are able your prayers are simply hypocritical piousness.

Jesus prayed at the tomb of Lazarus, but He also told the

disciples to *roll* away the stone, and then He *called* Lazarus from the grave.

Oh, friend, do you BACK UP YOUR PRAYERS? Do you do your part, and, having done your part, do you BELIEVE THAT GOD WILL KEEP HIS WORD? A lady came to me some time ago, greatly disturbed and said, "Doctor, I am so concerned about my son who is not saved. I lie awake all night long and weep my eyes out. I am so terribly worried I don't know what I shall do. I am so afraid he will be lost and I can't bear the thought. Oh, I pray, and pray, and pray, but I am so worried. Why doesn't God answer my prayer?" I replied, "God cannot answer your prayer under these conditions because you do not believe God. The Lord has said that it is NOT HIS WILL THAT ANY SHOULD PERISH. Do you believe that?" She replied, "Yes." I added, "And God also says that if we shall ask anything ACCORDING TO HIS WILL HE WILL DO IT. Do you believe that?" And she said, "Yes." Then I asked, "Well then, what are you worrying about? If you have the promise of God then stop fretting and begin praising God for what you BELIEVE HE IS GOING TO DO. When you ask God to save your son and then worry that God will not do it you are insulting Him. Go to Him and say, "LORD, I will not stop reminding You of Your promise but at the same time I thank Thee for what Thou hast promised to do,' and don't doubt any more." She saw the light. She dried her tears and said, "Thank You, Lord, I believe You will save my son. I will keep on praying but will never again doubt but that God will keep His word at His own good time." Several weeks later I received a letter beginning with, "Praise God, the Lord has answered my prayer and William has accepted Christ."

Friend, are your prayers unanswered because, while you pray, you are afraid that God will not answer your prayer? Jesus stood at the grave of Lazarus and said, *Father*, I thank thee that thou hast heard me. He thanked God in advance for the resurrection of Lazarus.

Friend, is the line up? Is the connection clear? Are you right with God and trusting Him? Then whatsoever ye shall ask of Him it shall be done.

Ere you left your room this morning
Did you think to pray?
In the Name of Christ the Saviour
Did you sue for loving favor
As your shield today?
Oh, how praying rests the weary,
Prayer will change your night to day;
So when life seems dark and dreary,
Don't forget to pray.

III

THE POWER OF PRAYER

Ask, and it shall be given you; seek, and ye shall find; knock, and it shall be opened unto you.
For every one that asketh receiveth; and he that seeketh findeth; and to him that knocketh it shall be opened (Luke 11:9-10).

We have been occupied with the science of Scriptural prayer and have studied the model prayer which the Lord Jesus Christ gave to His disciples when, after they had seen Him pray, they asked, *Lord, teach us to pray.* Now we shall see the unlimited power of believing prayer. *He that cometh to God must believe that he is, and that he is a rewarder of them that diligently seek him.* Prayer is not a matter of forcing God to do things for us but rather a coming to God in absolute faith that what we need will be given to us in answer to our prayers.

THREE ANSWERS TO PRAYER

The Lord ALWAYS answers believing prayer. He never fails when we come in faith to Him. But the Lord does not always answer our prayers in the same way or in the way that we desire. God is infinitely wise and sometimes finds it necessary to answer our petitions in the negative and say to us, "No, My child, what you ask for is not good for you, and so I will have to refuse your request." By-and-by you will understand the reason for it all.

When my children were small and I was practicing medicine there were many things about my office that looked very tempting and alluring to them and they wanted them badly. I remember that once one of the boys came running to me with a bottle of acid which he had found in the office and taken while I was not looking. He wanted that bottle above all things in the world. Nothing seemed more important at the moment than that bottle. So he asked "Daddy, Daddy, please, may I have this bottle?" Do you suppose I as a father answered his petition? I surely did, but not in the way that he had expected and wanted. Instead, I answered him tenderly yet firmly, "No, my child, you certainly cannot have it." He was too young to understand why, and so he began to sob and plead and beg and cry, but all to no avail, for, although I do not like to refuse my children anything they need, I love them too much to let them have anything which will hurt them, no matter how they may cry and beg and plead.

Thus does our Heavenly Father deal with us. He knows our frame. He knows what we need and what is best for us. Sometimes we come to Him and plead and beg for some precious thing — something that seems as dear as life itself. We do not see how we can ever get along without it. But He knows best, and in His precious love He sometimes refuses us the thing we want the most. Often we cannot understand why He takes away something, and our hearts are broken. But He looks ahead and in His wise plan He makes us weep by His refusal of our petition that He may spare us from something worse.

Oh, friend, are you grieving today because God has refused to give you that which you desired so much? Have you asked Him for something, and it has not been given to you? Then BELIEVE HIM that His plan is best. Remember that if we ask anything according to His will it shall be given. Then trust Him and rest in His wise decision. Can you do that and say:

> I will not doubt though all my ships at sea
> Come sailing home with tattered mast and sail;
> I will believe the hand that cannot fail
> From seeming evil worketh good for me;
> And though I weep because those sails are tattered,
> I still shall cry while my last hope lies shattered,
> "I'll trust in Thee."
> I will not doubt though all my prayers return
> Unanswered from the still white realm above;

I will believe it was an all-wise love
That has refused these things for which I yearn;
And though at times I cannot keep from grieving,
Still the pure ardor of my fixed believing
Undimmed shall burn.
I will not doubt though sorrows fall like rain
And troubles swarm like bees about a hive;
I will believe the heights for which I strive
Are only reached through anguish and through pain;
And though I writhe and groan beneath my crosses,
I still shall reap through my severest losses,
The greater gain.
I will not doubt; well anchored in this faith,
Like some staunch ship my soul braves every gale;
So strong its courage that it will not quail
To meet the mighty unknown sea of death.
Oh, may I cry while body parts with spirit,
"I will not doubt," so listening worlds may hear it,
With my last breath.

FIVE AVENUES OF POWER

There are in the possession of every believer five outlets of power. Although there is but one source of power, and that source is the Holy Spirit, there are these five channels through which we may exert the power of the indwelling and guiding Holy Spirit. These five outlets are as follows. I exert spiritual power by —

1. What I am among men.
2. What I say to men.
3. What I do before men.
4. What I give of my possessions.
5. What I dare to claim in the Name of Jesus.

The first four of these are limited in their scope by the very nature of the exercise. But the last of these five, the things I claim in Jesus' Name, is as infinite, omnipotent and omnipresent as God Himself. Through the avenue of believing prayer I can partake of the omnipotence of God and utilize His omnipresence.

BY WHAT I AM

I can greatly influence men by WHAT I AM. The influence of a godly man is felt even before he speaks. There is something about true godliness that you can feel the moment you enter the presence of a godly person. When a man is truly holy he does not need to go about bragging about it or telling you how long he has lived without sinning. When he tells you that he is already committing one of the worst sins in the world, "spiritual pride." The more holy we become, the more we realize our failings and sins. Humility and a deep consciousness of our unworthiness is the true mark of holiness and the mark of true holiness. The nearer we live to Him of whom the angels chant "Holy, Holy, Holy, Lord God almighty," the more we will confess our own sinfulness and rejoice in HIS HOLINESS. Men are not influenced by what we say nearly so much as by what we are. If my example is for good it reacts upon them. If it is bad the reverse is true.

BY WHAT I SAY

In addition to my influence among men through what I am, I can influence them by what I say. This is particularly true of the preacher, of course, but in a general way it is true of all believers. You can generally tell what a man is by his words. Words are but audible thoughts. What a man talks about he must think about first. If your conversation is chaste and pure it indicates a chaste and pure heart. It may be said of all of us as the damsel said of Peter on the night he betrayed the Lord, *Thy speech bewrayeth thee.*

One of the greatest evils in the Church today is the looseness of the tongue when dealing with sacred things. Too many Christians and officers and preachers tell jokes about the Bible or the characters in the Bible, speak lightly of the Devil and do not even shrink from telling questionable parlor stories, all of which only betrays what is in their heart. One who has reverence for the Word of God will not speak jokingly about the things in the Bible. And the folk who joke about the Devil have not yet learned what a fearful enemy he is. The all too common custom of many Christians, of speaking lightly about holy things, is encouraging disrespect for the Bible and holy things. Smutty and suggestive stories are absolutely out of place anywhere, and to tell them is a positive sin. A smutty tongue betrays a smutty heart. The man who will tell suggestive stories, even though called "parlor stories," is not safe to leave alone with decent women. If you want to know what a man thinks in his heart, just listen to what comes out of his mouth. *As he thinketh in his heart, so is he.*

But, on the other hand, what a power we can be if by our conversation and speech we lift men higher and tell them of the Lord Jesus Christ. It has pleased God by the foolishness of preaching to save them that believe. Faith cometh by hearing and hearing by the Word of God. God has been pleased to make the spoken word the medium for the transmission of the story of grace, and the ear the instrument for receiving it into the heart. How greatly therefore we can influence men by what we say for Jesus Christ. It is not in vain that Scripture says, *Let your speech be alway with grace, seasoned with salt, that ye may know how ye ought to answer every man.* And now, today, by the radio our ability to reach multiplied thousands has been enhanced beyond imagination. How the world uses the medium of speech and oratory to spread its propaganda! How active we should be to be even wiser than they are and to "buy up every opportunity" for letting men hear the message of salvation. God has still placed at our disposal this privilege of sending out the spoken word to the masses. When the privilege is denied us by-and-by we will probably be willing to give almost anything for the opportunity of which we now think so lightly.

BY WHAT I DO

The third avenue through which I am able to influence those about me is by the things I Do. Paul says that we are epistles read and known by all men. People study our actions far more than they listen to our words. Someone has said, "What you do speaks so loud that I cannot hear what you say." The world is very quick to detect the inconsistencies of the Christian. It sometimes is far more sensitive to the sins of believers than they are themselves. There may be many things that we do not think are wrong but if they constitute a stumbling block either in the way of a brother or to the world it becomes our duty to forego our liberty if need be, that our testimony may not be marred. Paul was willing to give up the eating of meat, not because he felt it was wrong, but because others were offended, and he was willing to sacrifice his privilege for the good of the testimony of Jesus Christ. A Christian who visits worldly places, copies worldly habits and practices worldly habits or seeks worldly pleasures may be not only hurting his own spiritual life but may be keeping others from coming to Christ. But when we live for Him then we become signboards for Him which will ever point men and women to the *Lamb of God, which taketh away the sin of the world.*

By What I Give

The fourth outlet of power and influence in my life is by what I am willing to give. We cannot all be preachers or missionaries, but we can all by our Scriptural giving support these ministries and thus influence people with the Gospel through our gifts in support of it.

Notice that all these four outlets of service are limited in their scope. *What I am* can only influence those with whom I came in contact. *What I say* can only influence those to whom I speak. By *what I do* I can influence only those whom I meet from day to day and contact in my daily walk. By *my giving* I can influence others, too, but my influence is limited by the income I have. Many of you would like to give a million dollars for the Gospel, but you have only five dollars. Most of us are sharply limited in the amount we can do by our gifts. But when we come to the fifth outlet of power we leave the realm of the limited and we enter the realm of the —

Omnipotent

Prayer leaps over all barriers, stops at no distances and balks at no obstacles because it is in touch with the infinite resources of heaven. By prayer I can get on my knees and visit the missionaries in Africa, China and the North Pole in a flash of time. When I lay hold of the line of prayer I can move heaven and remove mountains. Even with our fastest mail, it takes days to reach people on the other side of the world, but by prayer I can reach them by way of the throne of grace in a moment. Prayer is omnipotent. I remember calling on a very dear old saint of God, who was over eighty years of age. I rapped at the door and when she was slow in answering I feared something might have happened. But finally she came, and apologized for being a little slow by saying, "You see, when you rapped I happened to be in China, and I wanted to finish my business there first." I looked at her and wondered whether she had become childish and demented. But she was in her right mind as she continued, "You see, my son, every morning I take a trip around the world and visit the Christians in Asia and Europe, the missionaries in China and Africa, Japan and the islands of the sea. I visit them all and meet with them at the Mercy Seat."

Yes, it is real. Your loved ones may be in trouble a thousand miles away and you cannot reach them in time to aid them by your personal presence, and your material help may be days too late, but you can help them IMMEDIATELY by getting in touch with heaven. You can fly to them on the wings of prayer and bring down the omnipotence of heaven by the simple expedient of believing prayer.

Of all the outlets of power, only the outlet of prayer is omnipotent and omnipresent. How little can I give. How few I can reach with my words and by my life: But I can reach ALL men everywhere by prayer. How sad that we so often neglect this greatest of all sources of power! How little we pray, and how guilty we are of the indictment of James: *Ye have not, because ye ask not. Ye ask, and receive not, because ye ask amiss, that ye may consume it upon your lusts.*

LORD, TEACH US TO PRAY

What a friend we have in Jesus,
  All our sins and griefs to bear.
What a privilege to carry,
  Everything to God in prayer.
O what peace we often forfeit,
  O what needless pain we bear,
All because we do not carry
  EVERYTHING to God in prayer.

IV

HINDRANCES TO PRAYER

We have studied the negative and the positive elements of prevailing prayer. First we studied some of the things the Lord Jesus told His disciples NOT to do when they prayed. They were not to be like the hypocrites and not to follow their example of long, meaningless prayers. Furthermore, they were not to pray as do the heathen, whose prayers consist of the vain repetition of meaningless phrases and expressions. Prayer is more than the repeating of words. Prayer is the breath of the soul. Prayer is the establishing of a vital contact between the soul and God Himself through the medium of the Lord Jesus Christ. Then we studied the Model Prayer of our Lord Jesus. And finally we saw the OMNIPOTENCE and the OMNIPRESENCE of prayer. Now we shall consider some of the things which prevent the answer to our prayers.

We will not argue the matter as to whether God always hears and answers prayer. One Scripture will answer that question for us very readily:

> If any of you lack wisdom, let him ask of God, that giveth to all men liberally, and upbraideth not, and it shall be given him.
> BUT LET HIM ASK IN FAITH, NOTHING WAVERING.
> For he that wavereth is like a wave of the sea driven with the wind and tossed.
> For let not that man think that he shall receive any thing of the Lord (James 1:5-7).

FAITH AND PRAYER

This passage brings us face to face with the first hindrance to our prayer life. We do not ask in faith. It was the Lord Jesus who said, *According to your faith be it unto you.* The reason that many of our prayers are not answered is simply because we do not EXPECT GOD TO ANSWER them when we pray to Him. We ask God for certain things and then rise from our knees and keep right on worrying and fretting about the very thing we have prayed to Him about. Do you remember the story of Peter in the book of Acts? Peter, you recall, had been cast into prison.

The Christians in Jerusalem called a prayer meeting in one of the homes for Peter, and prayed to the Lord to deliver him. God did deliver him and loosed the bonds and sent an angel to lead him out. Then Peter went directly to the house where the prayer meeting was being held, and rapped at the door. But when they answered the knock they would not believe that it was Peter, and refused to let him in, for they supposed that it was an angel. Read the captivating story again in the twelfth chapter of Acts which tells how the young maiden Rhoda met Peter at the door and in her excitement let Peter stand outside while she rushed in to break up the prayer meeting; but they refused to believe her.

We are all too often just like that. If God were to answer our prayers we would be the most surprised people in the world. Listen, friend, the reason some of your prayers are not answered is because you do not believe that God will answer them. You have been praying for the salvation of that daughter and she is not yet saved. Do you have faith that God will answer that prayer? Then why are you so worried and anxious about it? Believe God is going to answer that prayer and begin thanking Him for it in advance. You have been praying about that husband of yours, but do you believe God will answer you? If you believe that, then why do you not rest in faith and see what God will do?

FAITH IS THE VICTORY THAT OVERCOMES THE WORLD
WE PRAY AMISS

In the fourth chapter of James we read in verses 2 and 3:

> Ye have not, because ye ask not. Ye ask, and receive not, because ye ask amiss, that ye may consume it upon your lusts.

Here is another reason for unanswered prayer. James says, *Ye ask, and receive not, because ye ask amiss, that ye may consume it upon your lusts. James says,* "You are too selfish in your prayers. You are too much concerned with SELF and not enough with HIM." Our object and purpose in prayer should always be THE GLORY OF GOD, and we should always pray in the WILL OF GOD. Too many times we want OUR way and not HIS way. We make our plans and then ask God to endorse them, instead of fitting ourselves into HIS plan.

SIN HINDERS PRAYER

A third hindrance to prayer is unconfessed sin in our lives. It is David who says:

> If I regard iniquity in my heart, the Lord will not hear me.

The force of that verse is this: "If I regard, fondle and tolerate unconfessed sin in my heart, God will not hear." The word "regard" implies toleration. Knowingly fostering sin or bitterness, and stubbornly refusing to yield it to the Lord will cause our prayers to go unanswered. James tells us:

> Confess your faults one to another, and pray one for another, that ye may be healed. The effectual fervent prayer of a righteous man availeth much.

Before there can be effectual and fervent prayer there must be confession of faults. Now that does not mean that we are to confess our sins in public or our private sins one to another. We confess our sins to God, but James states very clearly that we are to confess our FAULTS one to another. What a need of this there is in the Church today! How little of confession there is among Christians! The hardest three words in the world are still those three words, "I have sinned."

Perhaps there is in your heart, my friend, something that you KNOW is contrary to God's will and you KNOW that God has been dealing with you concerning this matter. Then listen to my advice. Stop praying. You are wasting your time. Get right with the Lord first and then you can do more in two minutes of praying than you are now accomplishing in a month.

ANSWERING YOUR OWN PRAYERS

Another reason why God does not answer some prayers is because God expects us to answer them ourselves. There are some prayers we are to answer and God will turn a deaf ear to all such petitions. Do not ask God to do anything for you that you can do yourself. Now I trust I will not be misunderstood. Before God will answer some prayers we must first do our part.

Picture a man who gets up and pleads with the Lord for a poor lost world. Let us suppose he is in a prayer meeting and for five minutes he stands praying to God to save poor lost men and women. Now all that seems very pious, but really the prayer never reaches the ceiling of the church. It goes little higher than the roof of his mouth. Do you know why?

During that very day this same man has met and rubbed shoulders with a hundred unsaved people and has never spoken to a single one concerning Christ. All day long he has been so busy gathering in the shekels that he has not witnessed to a single soul. He rode on the bus with an unsaved man and talked about the weather. He dealt for an hour with an unsaved salesman in the office and talked business but never said a word for Christ. He sat and visited with the neighbor while waiting for supper to be prepared and talked about fishing and the baseball games but never uttered a word about the man's soul. And then he goes to prayer meeting and prays God to save those whom he should have contacted for the Lord.

All such praying is merely a violent discharge of super-heated atmosphere. The farmer may pray for a good crop in the fall but unless he plows and drags and sows and cultivates, God will not answer his prayers. A person in an accident, bleeding from a severed artery, may say, "I believe God can heal me," and it may sound very pious, but unless a tourniquet is applied and a doctor called, if he is available, the person will bleed to death.

Our faith is a reasonable faith. If God has given us a remedy then we are to use it and not neglect His provision. I may pray the Lord to give me sufficient food but I have to work to provide it and then I have to eat it as well. There is much of foolish fanaticism concerning prayer and faith. But faith and works go together. Listen once more to James, as he speaks in chapter 2 beginning at verse 14:

> What doth it profit, my brethren, though a man SAY he hath faith, and have not works? can faith save him?
> If a brother or sister be naked, and destitute of daily food, And one of you say unto them, Depart in peace, be ye

warmed and filled; notwithstanding ye give them not those things which are needful to the body; what doth it profit?

Here is practical Christianity. What this poor brother and sister need is not super-pious phrases and prayers but something to eat, and if you are in a position to provide it and do not do it, then praying for them so you can keep your own purse full becomes, instead of a spiritual exercise, the most despicable and abominable hypocrisy. The world is waiting for a practical demonstration of the love of Christ in something more than pious talk and praying. If you walk into some poor brother's home and there is poverty and want, and you have in your possession the wherewithal to relieve that condition, then Do Not slip out of your responsibility by a pious "Let us pray about it." God wants you to do something about it, too, and then He will answer your prayer Through you.

I know a man who prays very fervently for the cause of missions and then drops a dime in the missionary offering afterwards. And yet that same man went fishing yesterday. He drove forty miles and used up a dollar's worth of gas and oil. He bought thirty-five cents' worth of hooks, paid five dollars for a boat, and fifteen cents for a soft drink on the way home. He caught twenty cents' worth of fish. And yet that man puts in one dime for missions and then soothes his conscience by doing a little extra praying!

Oh, my friend, I am not trying to offend anyone. I like to fish, too. I love it. But, brother, I would rather fish for souls than anything else. "Show me your faith without your works and I will show you my faith by my works," says James.

There is a great deal of cheapness and penuriousness and covetousness covered up by pious praying. Remember the Pharisees of Jesus' day. They made long prayers but devoured widows' houses. The fat old paunchy landlord who grinds the last penny out of the poor for exorbitant rent may hold a high position in the church and buy his way into the official family of the church and pray ever so piously, but certainly God will not hear him.

There are many other hindrances to prayer we might mention, but there is one which we must study for a moment. It is found in I Peter 3:7:

> Likewise, ye husbands, dwell with them [that is, the wives] according to knowledge, giving honour unto the wife, as unto the weaker vessel, and as being heirs together of the grace of life; THAT YOUR PRAYERS BE NOT HINDERED (I Peter 3:7).

Here is a hindrance to prayer that I fear has been altogether overlooked by many. Peter in this chapter is speaking of the conduct of husbands and wives and tells us that an inconsistent life in the home will cause our prayers to go unanswered or at least hindered. I know of no instruction more vitally needed than this. Many children are going to hell today because of the example in the home of professing Christian fathers and mothers. After all, the home is the one place where character is formed more than any other place in the world. You may send your children to school and Sunday school and catechism faithfully, but when they reach maturity they will reflect the atmosphere of the home above everything else. If there is quibbling and wrangling in the home do not expect your children to escape the sad influence.

Husbands, dwell with your wives according to knowledge; that is, sensibly. Recognize the fact that your wife is a peculiar vessel, different from a man and created for a different purpose. I speak as a physician. The years of my medical practice have taught me that countless homes are broken because the husband does not understand the peculiar function of woman. A woman is a mother at heart. Do not quench that desire. A woman is so constituted that she is periodically subject to physiological reactions and physical emotions over which she has little control. She goes through physiological and psychological crises that the male knows nothing of by experience. Recognize this fact. Sympathy, not criticism, is what she needs. She is the mother of your children and she bore all the pain, whereas yours is the pleasure that comes through fatherhood. Dwell then with her according to knowledge. She depends on you. The very time she seems to resent your love is the very time she needs it most. I am sure you understand what Peter means.

Mothers and fathers, the home you make for your children will determine in a large way what their eternal home will be. Never quarrel before your children. You should not quarrel at all, but if you do, NEVER, NEVER do it before your children. Nothing will wreck a young life like a quarrelsome home. Never let the sun go down upon a family squabble. Like snowballs, the farther they roll the larger they grow. What America needs today, if it is to survive is more godly, peaceful homes. Needed more than bigger armies and navies is the return of the home to the pattern of the Trinity. It is significant that the Being of God is patterned after a family. The Bible presents the Godhead as Father, Son and Holy Spirit. Although He is but one God, He is a FAMILY of Persons.

Parents, how much do you pray for your children? First, having set the example of a loving Christian husband and wife, how much have you prayed for your children? Nay, let me go further. How much do your children HEAR YOU pray for them?

God pity the child who grows up in a home where it never hears father and mother pray. God have mercy on you Christians who profess to know Christ and whose children never HEAR you pray for them. Oh, yes, you bow your head at mealtime and you call it prayer. But do you really pray, or are you only figuring out how much that heifer will bring?

I want to close this message with a testimony to my mother and father now in glory. Seldom was there a day that I did not hear Mother and Father pray for me. Oh, how she would plead, how she would cry to God for me as she mentioned me by name! And when, years afterward, God spoke to my heart and saved me, it was Mother's prayers which, next to God, had more to do with my conversion than everything else — more than all the preaching and teaching I had ever heard. It was Mother's prayers that followed me.

> 'Twas in the years of long ago when life was fair and bright
> And ne'er a tear and scarce a fear o'ercast my day or night
> That often in the eventide I found her kneeling there,
> And just one word, my name, I heard, my name in Mother's prayer

I thought but little of it then, though reverence touched my
  heart
For her whose love sought from above for me the better
  part,
But when the sterner battles came with many a subtle snare,
'Twas then one word, my name, I heard, my name in
  Mother's prayer.
I wandered on and heeded not God's oft-repeated call
To turn from sin to live for Him and give to Him my all,
Until at last of sin convinced I sank in deep despair,
My hope awoke when memory spoke my name in Mother's
  prayer.
That pleading heart, that soul so tired, has gone unto her
  rest,
But ere with me for aye shall be the memory of her trust;
And when I enter heaven's gates and meet her over there,
I'll praise the Lord for just one word, MY NAME, in Mother's
  prayer.

Oh, that some wayward soul might hear memory's call today,
and through Mother's prayer be brought to the feet of Christ!

CHAPTER 7

THE CHEMISTRY OF MATTER

According to the teaching of the Book, this old world on which we live today is not to continue in its present form, but is to undergo a purification by fire at the end of the ages. This is definitely and unmistakably taught in the Scriptures.

To the Christian, of course, the word of the Lord alone is enough, but we shall look both at the Scriptural teaching and the discoveries of scientists, to see how they also agree and harmonize. Both of these indicate with great certainty that the time is coming — and it may not be nearly as far off as scientists believe — when this old earth, 25,000 miles in circumference and 8,000 miles in diameter, will blow up like a bomb and be burned, to be recast into a new and rejuvenated world in which righteousness will forever dwell and sin shall never again be known. We might quote a score or more passages from the Book to support this assertion but we shall begin with the one which is the most definite and also the best known. It is found in II Peter 3 and the passage reads as follows:

> Knowing this first, that there shall come in the last days scoffers, walking after their own lusts, and saying, Where is the promise of his coming? for since the fathers fell asleep, all things continue as they were from the beginning of the creation.
> For this they willingly are ignorant of, that by the word of God the heavens were of old and the earth standing out of the water and in the water: Whereby the world that then was, being overflowed with water, perished.
> But the heavens and the earth, which are now, by the same word are kept in store, reserved unto fire against the day of judgment and perdition of ungodly men.
> But, beloved, be not ignorant of this one thing, that one day

116

is with the Lord as a thousand years, and a thousand years
as one day.
The Lord is not slack concerning his promise, as some
men count slackness; but is longsuffering to us-ward, not
willing that any should perish, but that all should come to
repentance.
But the day of the Lord will come as a thief in the night; in
the which the heavens shall pass away with a great noise,
and the elements shall melt with fervent heat, the earth also,
and the works that are therein shall be burned up.
Seeing then that all these things shall be dissolved, what
manner of persons ought ye to be in all holy conversation
and godliness,
Looking for and hasting unto the coming of the day of God,
wherein the heavens being on fire shall be dissolved, and
the elements shall burn with fervent heat?
Nevertheless we, according to his promise, look for new
heavens and a new earth, wherein dwelleth righteousness
(II Peter 3:3-13).

First of all, let me remind you that this is the word of the
Lord and not the word of man. It is God's word as truly as
John 3:16 is the word of God. In this passage we have God's
statement of the certainty of that event and it mentions two
great forces of nature; namely, FIRE AND WATER. To prove the
certainty that the world will be destroyed by FIRE, Peter recalls
the other time when the world was destroyed by WATER. Referring to the PAST judgment of the Flood, he adds, *The heavens
and the earth, which are* NOW, *by the same word (of God) are
made and are* STORED *with fire, reserved against the day of judgment and perdition. Stored with fire* is the literal translation.

FIRE AND WATER are the two most powerful forces in nature
and the two most useful forces in nature as well, for although
we think of them as opposites, like light and dark, dry and wet,
they nevertheless have much in common and are both man's
greatest allies in his struggle for existence. With waterpower
we turn great turbines to generate electricity by which we light
our homes and streets, run our factories, and turn the wheels
of industry. The same is true of fire. With fire we cook our
meals, heat our homes, run our steamships and railroads, fuse
precious metals, and melt them to be molded in any desired
form. Yet when these two forces get beyond man's control

what destruction results! What is more destructive than fire
and water when they burst their bonds? We think of the great
floods of our day and the fires that have leveled whole cities.
The greatest catastrophes of all history were the Flood of Noah
by WATER and the destruction by fire of the cities of the plain,
Sodom and Gomorrah.

Is it not therefore significant that the Lord Jesus in speaking of the end of the age uses these two very historical calami-
ties as illustrations? For in speaking of these days He says: *But
as the days of Noe were, so shall also the coming of the Son
of man be.* These two elements, fire and water, speak of JUDG-
MENT. They were God's instruments of destruction in the two
greatest earth judgments in history and are used as figures of
the still greater judgment to come.

Yes, the earth was once destroyed by WATER and it shall
yet be once more destroyed by FIRE. This is what GOD says.
It will not make any difference whether you believe it or not
so far as its certainty is concerned, but it will make a great
difference to YOU whether you believe it or not so far as your
own ESCAPE from the fire of His judgment is concerned. Remember, it is WHAT GOD says that counts, and not what you
think. So we will turn now to the sure Word of God and then
to the testimony of scientists, and may God help you to believe it.

Turning to II Peter 3, we read first of all the occasion for
this revelation. Listen to the third verse: *Knowing this first, that
there shall come in the last days scoffers, walking after their
own lusts, and saying,* WHERE IS THE PROMISE OF HIS COMING?
In the last days scoffers shall come laughing at our preaching
of the Coming of the Lord and the ensuing judgments. Are we
living in those days now? Has there ever been a time when
there was more scoffing at the Word of God? Even professing
Christendom has to a great extent given up its belief in the
literal Return of the Lord Jesus Christ and the end of the world.
I am fully conscious of the fact that my message is not popular
with the masses, but, thank God, I am not seeking to be popular
with men but with THE MAN in the glory who called me to
preach the Word.

Now to all of you who doubt this Word, Peter calls attention to the fact that once before men were told that God would destroy the world. This time it was by water and then as today men would not believe God's servants, and rejected the preaching of NOAH, but THE FLOOD CAME JUST THE SAME! All the unbelievers perished and only Noah and his house were saved because they believed the word of the Lord. "Listen," says Peter, "let this be a warning to you who scoff and reject the Word!" Then he adds in verses 5, 6 and 7:

> For this they willingly are ignorant of, that by the word of God the heavens were of old and the earth standing out of the water and in the water:
> Whereby the world that then was, being overflowed with water, perished:
> But the heavens and the earth, which are now, by the same word are kept in store, reserved unto fire against the day of judgment and perdition of ungodly men.

What a word of warning! "Remember the flood," says Peter. God waited then also, for years, because He did not want men to perish, but finally after years of long-suffering on the part of GOD IT CAME. I suppose that while Noah was building the Ark many a "wisecrack" was made and many a "wag" shook his head and tapped his skull as he said, "Look at that old fool getting ready for the Flood and building a ship on dry land with not a cloud in sight." But old Noah kept right on hammering just as I am going to do, in spite of all the jeering and scoffing of unbelievers. Then THE FLOOD CAME.

Peter says, "Scoffers shall come in the last days also." They are here now in ever increasing numbers. A group of men, otherwise kind to me, burst into hilarious laughter when I told them in a hotel lobby in Detroit that all the efforts of man to bring about peace and Utopia without the Coming of the Lord Jesus Christ, were doomed to failure. "Why," said one of them, "do YOU believe that Christ is coming back?" They burst into laughter at my unqualified belief in the Bible, and when the laughter subsided one remarked, "Oh, yes, I heard He was coming on a white horse. I suppose He will stop in Kentucky to pick out a good one." Another said, "Well, if Jesus Christ is coming

back again He has been on the way a long time and He is
mighty slow. Maybe His horse got the blind staggers." Then
they all laughed again. I left them but not until I had quoted
II Peter 3:3, saying, "Now I know that He is near, for Peter
tells me that when men scoff like this then we are in the very
last days." *Knowing this first that there shall come in the last
days scoffers.* Yes, the Word of the Lord is true.

Having answered these scoffers, Peter then turns to the Christians and reassures and encourages them in the following verses:

> But, beloved, be not ignorant of this one thing, that one day
> is with the Lord as a thousand years, and a thousand years
> as one day.
> The Lord is not slack concerning His promises, as some
> men count slackness; but is longsuffering to us-ward, not
> willing that any should perish, but that all should come to
> repentance (II Peter 3:8, 9).

Notice the words. The Lord has delayed His Coming because
He wants men to be saved before He comes, knowing that after
He comes, those who have rejected His offer willfully will have
no other opportunity. God gave the people before the Flood
many years to repent, and He has done and is doing the same
thing Now. But this delay will not continue forever. Peter says
in the next verse:

> THE DAY OF THE LORD WILL COME as a thief in the night;
> in the which the heavens shall pass away with a great noise,
> and the elements shall melt with fervent heat.

This description includes both the judgments which will ac-
company His Second Coming and also the final purification by
fire at the end of the Millennium. Both are spoken of here but
we are interested more particularly in the fact and the nature
of the destruction, than in the element of time and its duration.
The heavens shall pass away with a great noise. In the original
we have the suggestion of a tremendous explosion which will
produce this great noise. Now the word "heavens" as used here
does not refer to the heaven where God dwells. There are at least
three heavens mentioned in the Scriptures: the atmospheric
heavens, referring to the atmosphere surrounding the earth with

its clouds and vapors; the starry heavens; and the third heaven or the abode of God.

From the use of the word "heavens" here we know that Peter is speaking particularly of the atmospheric heavens but also of the starry heavens. Let us think for the present of the atmospheric heavens or the air around the earth. This heaven, says Peter, will explode with a great noise. Then he adds that the elements shall burn with a fervent heat. This means the elements of which the earth is composed. There are over one hundred of these elements known to chemists of which terrestrial matter is composed. We are familiar with a number of them, such as oxygen, hydrogen, calcium, potassium, sodium, iron, magnesium, tin, gold, silver, copper, etc. So great will be the heat of the exploding heavens that the minerals and ores of this earth will melt, fuse and run together.

Then follows the third event, according to Peter. The earth and the works that are therein shall be dissolved and burned up. What a conflagration! It would be hard to imagine were it not that God Himself says it is going to happen. Oh, men and women, hear the Word of the Lord and prepare against that day when the Lord shall arise to punish terribly the earth, and judge those who have rejected His Word.

We have all been shocked by the reports in the papers and over television of the bombings in war zones. We have seen the pictures of the burning villages and cities as the flames swept over acres and acres of buildings. Yet this is but child's play with rubber toys compared with that blast which will occur when God touches off the elements and the heavens shall explode with a great noise. The Bible says the moon shall turn RED by the reflected light of the conflagration. Think of that for a moment. The moon will turn to blood. Though it is thousands of miles away, so great will be the conflagration of this old world that the reflection of the flames will make the moon turn red. The sun shall be darkened. The smoke of this explosion will leap countless miles into space until it envelopes the sun, which is 93,000,000 miles away, and turns it as black as sackcloth. So great will be the explosion that the shock of it will disturb the stars millions and millions of miles away and cause them to be diverted in their courses as though they fell from heaven. It will be the crash of worlds about which the scientists have dreamed.

The whole Word of God corroborates this revelation of Peter. All through the Old Testament as well as the New we have this prophecy. Let me read two or three of them. Here is one from Joel 2:30-31:

> And I will shew wonders in the heavens and in the earth, blood, and fire, pillars of smoke.

The expression "pillars of smoke" probably refers to huge columns of smoke leaping countless miles into space, for immediately after the mention of the pillars of smoke we read:

> The sun shall be turned into darkness, and the moon into blood.

Or listen to Isaiah 13:9-11:

> Behold, the day of the Lord cometh, cruel both with wrath and fierce anger, to lay the land desolate; and he shall destroy the sinners thereof out of it.
> For the stars of the heaven and the constellations thereof shall not give their light: the sun shall be darkened in his going forth, and the moon shall not cause her light to shine.
> And I will punish the world for their evil, and the wicked for their iniquity.

Let Ezekiel 32:7-8 speak:

> I will cover the heaven, and make the stars thereof dark; I will cover the sun with a cloud, and the moon shall not give her light.
> All the bright lights of heaven will I make dark over thee, and set darkness upon thy land, saith the Lord God.

Listen to the words of gentle Jesus in Matthew 24:29:

> Immediately after the tribulation of those days shall the sun be darkened, and the moon shall not give her light, and the stars shall fall from heaven, and the powers of heaven shall be shaken.

This shaking will undoubtedly be the means of disturbing the stars in their courses and making them fall from their places.

Let us add a quotation from Hebrews 12:25-27:

See that ye refuse not him that speaketh. For if they escaped not who refused him that spake on earth, much more shall not we escape, if we turn away from him that speaketh from heaven:

Whose voice then shook the earth: but now he hath PROMISED, saying, Yet once more I shake not the earth only, but also heaven.

And this word, Yet ONCE MORE, signifieth the removing of those things that are shaken, as of things that are made, that those things which cannot be shaken may remain.

Now do you doubt His Word? Do you question these Scriptures given by the Almighty Himself? If you doubt, my friend, you are neither wise nor scientific. Do not geologists tell us that their findings indicate a great cataclysmic upheaval many years in the past? an upheaval that removed islands and shifted continents? Do you doubt the record of God's Word? Then listen to scientists, for they are just as emphatic on this matter as the Bible. Peter, however, was 2,500 years ahead of modern scientists.

Bear in mind that Peter mentions three realms where this destruction will occur; namely, the heavens, the elements and the earth. Let scientists tell us about the heavens, that is, the atmosphere about the earth.

The air, the stuff we breathe to keep alive, is chiefly composed of two elements: oxygen and nitrogen, two of the most combustible gases in the world. Oxygen is the element needed for all combustion. Burning is merely the uniting of other elements and oxygen, with the resultant discharge of power and heat. We call this process "combustion" and oxygen is the one element needed for combustion. If you shut off the oxygen the fire goes out. If you add oxygen it flares up. Whether the slow combustion of your tissues or the more rapid combustion in an engine the process is the same.

The second element is NITROGEN. This is the one element which forms the base for many of our high explosives. It is nitrogen which makes dynamite explosive, nitrogen which makes TNT, and nitrogen of which nitroglycerin is composed. The air is made up of these two highly combustible elements. By God's providence they are present in such form that they do not explode, but cannot He who made these elements and the laws that keep them from exploding also so combine them so that they will explode? Man can do it on a small scale, utilizing only an infinitesimal percentage of the whole. Do you not see that when God says the heavens will explode with a great noise that the two elements necessary for this explosion are already present and have been all the time? When God gets ready to fulfill II Peter 3 He will have no difficulty!

Now look at the second thing Peter mentions. The elements shall melt with fervent heat. Every element known can be melted. If we could unlock the secret of molecular power we could make them fuse themselves. With some elements we have already been able to do this. I remember well that when I was a student in chemistry at the University of Illinois we made certain experiments in the laboratory with metallic sodium. Sodium is one of the best known and commonest of all elements. Table salt is one-third sodium and it is found in most of the foods we eat. However, metallic sodium, that is, sodium by itself and not in combination with other elements, is a grayish, moderately soft, puttylike substance. To preserve it in its metallic state it must be kept in kerosene or it will explode. If we take but a little piece of this sodium and throw it on water it will begin to sizzle and skip about on the surface and soon burst violently into flame by the heat of its own generation. You need no fire to light it. Simply throw it in water and it will catch fire. The contact of the sodium with water which is composed of two parts of hydrogen and one part oxygen, liberates this free hydrogen with such force that the heat produced causes the nascent hydrogen to ignite and burst into flame.

The world is two-thirds water on the surface and by volume much more. Water is H_2O, that is, two molecules of hydrogen and one molecule of oxygen. Each one of these elements is highly combustible. We have already referred to oxygen. Hydrogen is highly explosive and was once used in dirigibles, but because of the explosions caused by it, it is no longer used. Helium is sought instead for this purpose. Water is a combination of these two highly combustible elements and when God sets the world on fire He will have oceans of materials with which to do it. The sea is one vast reservoir of hydrogen and oxygen, a vast reservoir of fuel, as is also every lake, pond and river. Yet strangely enough these two elements in the combination of water are the natural enemy of fire and we use water to put out a blaze. What a wonderful Creator our God is!

Then, too, scientists tell us of that unknown quantity "ATOMIC FORCE," and a great deal of experimenting is being done with "atom smashing" apparatus in these days. Machines are being invented which aim at liberating the force that holds atoms together. It is maintained that the atomic force in the atoms of an ordinary five-cent piece if released suddenly would be powerful enough to blow up the greater part of the city of New York, leaving a crater hundreds of feet deep. Such are the discoveries of modern scientists. Do you doubt then that God who made the atoms and the worlds will be able to make the heavens explode and the elements burn with fervent heat? What fools men are who doubt the God of science. Then Peter adds:

> The earth also and the works that are therein shall be burned up.

Scientists tell us that it is a wonder this has not already happened and reminds us that astronomers know of at least eighteen stars which have blown up and disintegrated. This earth, we are told, is formed much like a globular egg with a shell and liquid contents. The shell constitutes the solid casing on which we live and is as thick in proportion as the shell of an egg to its semi-liquid contents. This outer solid shell of the earth varies in thickness, but, this thickness is nowhere believed to be more than a few hundred miles, and beneath this is a liquid core of molten elements at a temperature of approximately 1,500 degrees Fahrenheit. The whole interior of the earth is a mass of boiling, molten elements, gases and fire in a constant state of boiling at this tremendous temperature.

Again and again some of this mass bursts forth upon the surface through volcanoes, accompanied by terrible shakings of the earth which produce tidal waves. Millions upon millions of tons of molten sulphur and lava and melted elements have belched forth, inundating whole cities, and great clouds of smoke and volcanic ash obscured the face of the sun and the moon so that ships a thousand miles away reported their decks covered with the dust of the eruption. Certainly we need no further proof of the scientific statement that the earth is a seething caldron within. Think of the hot springs of water. Think of the Valley of a Thousand Smokes in Alaska. Some time ago an article appeared in *The National Geographic* describing this valley and giving pictures of the thousands of vents in its valley floor — vents from which superheated gases hissed forth, so hot that a green branch of a tree two inches in thickness was charred in a few seconds when held above it.

Miners digging into the earth tell us that as they go down it gets cooler for a certain distance and then below a certain level the temperature begins to rise rapidly so that very soon artificial cooling must be resorted to in order to carry on the work. But why go on? If you still do not believe, there is little hope for you. So much for the testimony of scientists. Now we will go back to Peter. Nineteen hundred years ago Peter said, under the inspiration of the Holy Spirit, *But the heavens and the earth, which are now, by the same word are kept in store, reserved unto fire against the day of judgment and perdition of ungodly men.* Why has it not blown up before? Because God says He is reserving it for the Day of Judgment.

What a solemn thought all this is! As we look upon the world today with all its progress, its great engineering feats, its colossal buildings and massive architecture, it is difficult to think that some day, and who knows how soon, all this will be destroyed in that great explosion. No wonder then that Peter, seeing all this, adds these words:

> Seeing then that all these things shall be dissolved, what manner of persons ought ye to be in all holy conversation and godliness,
> Looking for and hasting unto the coming of the day of God, wherein the heavens BEING ON FIRE shall be dissolved, and the elements shall burn with fervent heat? (II Peter 3:11-12).

What solemn thought! How serious we ought to be in view of all this. How we, as Christians, ought to set our affections on things which will not perish. In the light of all this is it any wonder that Jesus said:

> Lay not up for yourselves treasures upon earth, where moth and rust doth corrupt, and where thieves break through and steal:
> But lay up for yourselves treasures in heaven, where neither moth nor rust doth corrupt, and where thieves do not break through nor steal.

Oh, you rich men and women, remember that all that which you are amassing, you are gathering only for the burning. You who live for wealth, pleasure, and enjoyment and forget God, your labors shall all be burned up and you with them. I do not know where hell is, and I do not know a great deal about it, but I do know two things and these are: First, that God has plenty of material in this old world alone to make a hell when He sets it on fire (I often wonder if the fires of hell will not be kindled by the fires of the explosion of this old earth); second, that I shall never go there when that awful explosion takes place. The wicked will be there, as you have already noted in the many passages from the Word I have quoted in this message. Perhaps the wicked will be caught in that very explosion and be blown directly by it into the Lake of Fire.

I would not close my message in this manner, however. There is a way out and after all "the way out" is the message I want you to hear. Peter, you will notice, says a very strange thing in verse 12 of this chapter. He says to us, *Looking for and hasting unto the coming of the day of God, wherein the heavens being on fire shall be dissolved, and the elements shall melt with fervent heat.* How could Peter say of that awful day that we are LOOKING FOR AND HASTENING UNTO IT?

There can be only one answer and that is that Peter MUST HAVE KNOWN that he and we who have trusted the Lord Jesus Christ as our Saviour have nothing to fear by the coming of that day. That is exactly the case. Before that great and terrible Day of God shall come, believers shall all be caught out and taken to glory with the Lord for *God hath not appointed us to wrath.* Every blood-bought believer will have been with Him for at least a thousand years before that FINAL explosion occurs. We may probably witness that great conflagration and crash of worlds, but it will be from the safe retreat of the third heaven while we are in the presence of God — far, far away from the awful scene of destruction. This is certain from the verse that follows, in II Peter 3:13:

> Nevertheless we, according to his promise, look for new heavens and a new earth, wherein dwelleth righteousness.

A new heaven and a new earth! This does not mean a new heaven where God dwells but a renewed atmospheric heaven and earth. This destruction does not mean annihilation. Burning never annihilates, but merely changes the form of the substance and purifies it. When you burn a house it is destroyed but the elements composing it are not annihilated. They are still all in existence in the form of ash and soot and smoke and other products of combustion. Somewhere on this earth they still exist and may ultimately be taken up again by plants and trees to form new wood to be made into another house. There is no destruction of matter but merely a change in form. I may take a gold vase that is very worn and marred, dented and stained, and put it through the fire till it is all melted and the vase is destroyed, but the artisan can take that material now far purer than before, and recast and mold it into another vase far more beautiful than the first.

Thus God will do with the earth. He will burn it with fire only to bring out of it a NEW heavens and a NEW earth. The earth was defiled by man's sin and so must be purified. The atmospheric heavens were defiled by Satan and the fallen angels, for that is their domain under the prince of the power of the air, and so the atmosphere must be cleansed and purified. Out of it will come a better and more beautiful heavens and earth where sinners will never dwell and from which Satan shall be forever banished. We will spend ETERNITY in that new earth and heaven where there will be no sorrow, no pain, no suffering, no sickness, no death and, best of all, no more sinning and stumbling. There we shall be united with our loved ones forever and ever to enjoy His blessed presence.

But what a sad outlook for those who have not accepted the

Lord Jesus Christ. They shall be cast out forever into the place of eternal torment, into the place Jesus described as a place where the worm never dies and the fires never go out. And do you know why that day has not yet come? Peter says it is to give you another opportunity to be saved; to make possible for you, poor sinner, a little more time to flee for refuge to the Lord Jesus, for, in the last verse we shall mention in this chapter, Peter says, *And account that the long-suffering of our Lord is salvation.*

The long-suffering of God is salvation. God is waiting now for you to come before it is too late. He is holding back the fires of judgment because He wants YOU to be saved. Oh, will you come NOW? Now, before the door is eternally shut to you and you are plunged into the fires that cannot be quenched? Here is the way to come: BELIEVE ON THE LORD JESUS CHRIST. Bow your head and say, "Save me now, Lord Jesus." Then trust His Word which says that *Whosoever shall call upon the name of the Lord shall be saved.* This is His promise. Come now before it is too late.

CHAPTER 8

THE CHEMISTRY OF TEARS

The subject of this message is not a very pleasant one and yet it is one that is freighted with a great deal of comfort and joy in spite of its unpleasant associations. We refer to the subject of TEARS. In speaking of this subject we are dealing with something which is familiar to one and all; for from infancy to old age the record of every man's life is written in letters of tears. We might speak on a multitude of subjects with which only a few people are familiar but when we speak of tears all of us immediately recall the experiences of our own past life.

The Bible, too, is a book that has a great deal to say about the matter of tears. In it we see infants weeping, strong men weeping, and even the tears of the Saviour are mentioned on various occasions. The first time tears are mentioned in the Book is in II Kings 20:5. Here we have the record of a king weeping. Hezekiah is sick unto death and has just been informed by the Prophet that he is to die. Turning his face to the wall, he sobs out to the Lord in his plea for life and in answer to those tears the Lord stays the hand of death and adds years unto his life. The last mention of tears in the Bible is a more pleasant picture. It is found at the end of the Bible and we read in Revelation 21:4 these gracious words:

And God shall wipe away all tears from their eyes.

God is a great tear-drier. He dried the tears of a king in Israel's day when he cried to the Lord and at the end of time He will again wipe away ALL tears. Between these two verses we have the record of a living God, like a tender Father wiping away the tears of His erring children. There is not a living human being who does not need this drying of tears. All who read these words have shed tears at some time or another and the great majority have shed many, many tears. The shedding of tears is a peculiarly unique human method of expressing emotions, such as sorrow, pain, despair and disappointment. Man is the only created being who can laugh. Man, too, is the only one who can shed tears in the sense of expressing emotion. Other animals have tear glands and ducts but they are not used to give expression to the soul. Their only function is that of lubricating the eyeball.

We usually think of tears as a part of our physical frame but in reality I think of the tears and the glands that secrete them as organs of the soul rather than of the body. Tears have far more to do with the soul than with the body. More tears are shed from the pain that cuts the soul than those that afflict the body. The hottest tears are not those which come as the mother in her birth pangs gives life to her babe but rather when her heart is broken by the waywardness of the very one for whom she gave her life.

And now because we have said this, and because of the commonness of tears in all of our lives it is entirely fitting that we should ask the question: "Just what is a tear?" The chemist will tell you that a tear is a solution of sodium chloride and calcium and some other chemicals in an aqueous solution. The physiologists tell us that a tear is the lubricating fluid of the eyeball, secreted by the lachrymal glands and poured over the eyes to keep them from becoming dry. The Stoic says that a tear is a sign of human weakness and cowardice, and that real humans do not shed tears. The Epicurean says that tears are useless and we should eat and drink and be merry for tomorrow we die and there will be time enough to weep. Others say a tear is like pain — only an idea and imagination. They are neither salt nor wet but are all "in the head."

Now permit me to give you my own definition of a tear — looked at in its fullest meaning. A tear is a distillation of the soul. It is the deepest longing of the human heart in chemical solution. It is the concentrated extract; the final precipitate of the deepest feelings of the heart, filtered through the sieve of trial and testing. True tears are not camouflage but the PICTURE OF THE SOUL on the CANVAS OF THE EMOTIONS. They are the portraits of our deepest aspirations.

If tears are then so common and important, we ask the question, "Just what is the use of tears anyway?" They are so common an experience, that we ought to know. To illustrate what a valley of tears we are living in, I have made use of a little mathematical calculation in an effort to give you an idea of the immensity of the subject we are discussing. Suppose that every individual in the world sheds fifty tears a year. I realize this is far below the actual fact. Few if any shed less; almost all of us shed more. Some shed literal buckets full, but we shall take one tear a week as our starting figure. That means that in the world, with its two billion population, ONE HUNDRED BILLION tears are shed each year. Since there are about 420 drops to the ounce this would be 250 million ounces. Reduced to gallons it equals two million gallons and reduced to barrels it means forty thousand barrels. A barrel is three feet long; so laid end to end, these barrels of tears would reach twenty-four miles. In the last thousand years it would be twenty-four thousand miles or once around the world. Since the day of Adam it would mean six barrels laid side by side encircling the whole world. Figure it out for yourself. If all these tears could be barreled and poured into a canal from New York to San Francisco they would make a river in which barges could be floated.

Think of the sorrow in each tear. Think of the sorrow in the tear of the babe as it weeps hot, scalding tears over a broken toy or trinket. Think of the tears of the youthful lover — jilted by the dream of his life. Think of the tears of the young mother as she stands by the empty crib and moves over to the little casket and feels for the first time what sorrow really is. Think of the tears of the middle-aged mother as she stands at the station to see her son — perhaps her only son — sent away to the penitentiary for a crime against society. Hear her sob amidst those blinding tears, "Oh, if I could only have shed these tears over his casket when he was a baby, it would have been easier than this."

Think of the tears of the old white-haired man with friends

and comforts gone, standing at the brink of the dark unknown, and facing the darkness. He looks back and sees along the road of life the shattered fragments of a thousand hopes and longings. Those senile eyes can hardly shed a tear but as the last step draws nearer I see one tear glistening in the light of the fast setting sun and soon he is gone and the tear-soaked world rolls gaily on.

Think of the tears of the sinner as, convicted of the error of his way, he makes, as David says, *his bed to swim in tears.* Think of this river of tears. And in every tear a broken heart, a shattered home, a forsaken hope, and a blessing hand. "Why! Oh why! all these tears?" we may justly ask. This is a question, my friend, we shall try to answer.

MANY KINDS OF TEARS

Let us ask first of all, "What causes tears and what are they good for, anyway?" The first thing with which we associate tears, of course, is physical pain. This is usually the cause of the first tear that is ever shed in the life of mortal men. Before consciousness of sorrow and trials of the soul have come to the infant in the cradle, it will shed tears of pain because of some discomfort, a maladjustment of its clothing, hunger or even an open safety pin. These tears continue all through life from the cutting of the first tooth to the losing of the last aching stub. Physical pain through disease and accident are all too common.

But the hottest, sharpest, biting tears are not those caused by physical pain but because of a pain which is more deeply seated and rooted in the soul than the body. Ah, the very word — SORROW. What a world of meaning there is pent up in that word! And yet few realize truly what sorrow really is. Sorrow of the heart and the soul is the great tear-manufacturer.

There is the shallow sorrow over the loss of transient things. I remember occasions when the shedding of tears was laughable. Memory brings back to me an old man over seventy sitting in his kitchen weeping hot tears. So deep was his agony that I, as a preacher, was called to comfort him. When I arrived, his whole body was quaking with grief. He was a man in comfortable circumstances. He and his wife had accumulated a fortune of about forty thousand dollars as a result of hard work and penurious living. Then he had made an investment of five hundred dollars in a spurious concern and he had just found out that his five hundred dollars was gone. What grief he registered. How he wept over that loss of his paltry five hundred. All my attempts to comfort him by stating that it represented only a small fraction of his fortune and even hinting at the fact that he was over seventy years old with no children, and the residue of his estate would only be divided among a group of second cousins who were already wishing he would soon die, was of no avail. All he moaned was, "We worked so hard for it, and we may need it if bad times come." *Poor, poor rich man,* I thought. There will be tears that will some day sparkle as jewels in heaven, but these never will. We have little sympathy for such tears.

There are also the tears caused by thwarted love — the tears of the young lover who had built all the hopes of his life and woven all his dreams about the girl of his imagination, only to see them shattered in a moment through the fickleness of the human heart. I am thinking now of the tears of a mother over the lost love of a child, the child she nourished and prayed for and for whom she would happily have died. But he went into a world of sin and left her. Do you, young man, remember those tears as you left her — rivers of tears which flowed until no more tears could come? Can you think of those tears now, young man or woman away from home, without feeling something tugging at your heart which tells you that now is the time, before Mother is gone, to write to her and go to her and make right in a measure the cause of those tears?

Oh, if there is a son or a daughter listening to me who has a mother like that, STOP, STOP! and think now of the tears that are falling for you — tears which no chemist or alchemist can analyze and no philosopher can fathom! Oh, the SORROWFUL TEARS of a brokenhearted mother! Years ago I heard a song on a phonograph. I do not know who wrote it or sang it, but I do remember the words. They went something like this:

'So you're going to leave the old home, Jim. Today you're
   going away,
You're going among the city folks to dwell,'
So spoke a dear old mother to her boy one summer's day.
'If your mind's made up that way, I wish you well.
The old home will be lonely; I will miss you when you're
   gone;
The birds won't sing as sweet when you're not here;
But if you are in trouble, Jim, just write and let us know.'
She spoke these words and wept a sad good-bye.
'When troubles overtake you, when old companions shake
   you
As through this world you wander all alone;
When of friends you haven't any, in your pockets not a
   penny,
There's a mother always waiting you at home, sweet home.'
Ten years later to the village came a stranger no one knew;
His step was halt and ragged clothes he wore;
The little children laughed at him as down the lane he
   walked;
At last he stopped before a cottage door.
He gently knocked, no sound he heard. He thought *can she
   be dead?*
But soon he heard a voice well-known to him;
'Twas Mother's voice; her hair was silver white, the bleach
   of tears.
She cried, 'Thank God, they've brought me back my Jim.'
When troubles overtake you, when old companions shake
   you
As through this world you wander all alone,
When of friends you haven't any, in your pockets not a
   penny,
There's a mother always waiting you at home, sweet home.

Ah, what sadness results, when the tears of a mother's love
are spurned. No ink can write the message. No tongue can
tell the story.

There are also the tears of despair. After a brave but losing
struggle the last bit of courage is gone. And then we see the
last chance go. The soul has struggled so bravely but now
crumples at last. There are the tears of remorse which Jesus
tells about when they who have rejected His offer of mercy
shall find themselves cast out where there shall be weeping
and wailing and gnashing of teeth, knowing that once the door

stood open but is now forever shut, and that now they must enter the cave where the tracks lead ever in but never out. We might continue by discussing the causes of tears but we want to speak of another even more important matter.

THE PURPOSE OF TEARS

What is the use of tears, anyway? Are they not, after all, useless? Can a child by weeping repair its toy? Can a mother by crying get her child back from the dead? Can a soul by weeping and wailing and gnashing of teeth open again the doors of hell and find a way out? Certainly NOT. And yet tears are an indispensable part of our being.

First of all, tears MAKE US WILLING TO LEAVE this valley of tears when the time shall come some day. For there is not a thing which will make a man ready and willing to leave this world any sooner than trouble and tears. If there were no trouble or sorrow and no tears in the world, all of us would be perfectly content to remain here forever. We would say, "Let well enough alone, if YOU want to gamble and speculate about a future life, well and good, but since there are no tears here, I am willing to take a lease on life for ten thousand years." But now things are different. There are tears. You have wept over others who have gone before. You remember the tears which fell when your loved ones went away, and now and again, though life may be sweet, that strange, homesick feeling sweeps over you — that feeling which makes you sometimes long to go where they are and be free from doubt and tears forever, and be reunited with those loved ones you cannot forget.

Yes, life may be sweet, but we would not live always. We cannot think of never seeing them again. All of us who know the Lord and the emptiness of this world and the realities of eternity come sooner or later to the time when we say, "I am tired and weary. Now I want to go." How often I have witnessed this in Christians as the shadows began to fall. I have seen the wistful longing light in their eyes when, after years of toil and suffering, they looked forward to that place where *God shall wipe away all tears from their eyes.*

Tears also make us feel our dependence upon God. King

Alfonso once said that if he had been God he could have made a better creation than God did. What a pity that Alfonso was not present at creation! I do not know what God will do when some men die. They know so much more than God. For God has so clearly revealed Himself and yet men will take that Word and tear it in pieces and set up a puny puerile philosophy of their own. Like King Alfonso, they are not satisfied with the way God is doing things — they can do it better — UNTIL TEARS COME AND SORROWS COME.

When all else fails, many a man has seen God through the prism of tears who never saw Him in the sunlight. You can tell by a man's prayers whether he has shed few or many tears. Two men may be equally sincere in their prayers, but the one has learned a different dependence upon God. Some have been in the school of tears. And you can tell it by the very cadence and phraseology of their devotions. Before a man has had much trouble, his prayers are poetic and stereotyped, and he begins way up there with the sun and the moon and the stars and gives the Lord a great deal of astronomical information which must be very gratifying to the Almighty. Gradually, he comes down to the fleecy clouds, down over fields of green and gardens of gold, skipping over the hilltops into the meadows and finally alights with a flourish and a grand and glorious "World without end, AMEN."

But listen to that man after he has been through the furnace of affliction and has been bathed in the fountain of tears. Listen to him after his prayers have been sprayed with the heaven-sent dew of weeping. It is then a different story. Gone are the flights of poesy and prayer is now a laying hold of God. Perhaps it is not so beautiful as before, but power is there. The more beautiful of the two prayers offered by the Pharisee and the publican in the Temple was not that of the Pharisee, but of the repentant publican. Prayer is not telling God how much you have found out about Him, but a consciousness that He already knows all about you.

Another reason for tears is that it teaches us the much needed grace of sympathy. In olden times, priests were set aside for their office by having water sprinkled on their hands and head and feet, but today to be fitted for the office of comfort and sympathy, we must first be baptized in the baptism of tears. To those of you who have never felt the sorrow over the loss of loved ones, these words call to you to take your shoes from off your feet, for the place whereon we tread now is HOLY GROUND. If you have never wept over loved ones gone, these words will mean little to you, for sympathy is born in travail and in tears.

I used to try and comfort people and preach comforting funeral sermons, and sometimes, as I go back and remember those days, I wonder why people did not throw me out. It was before I had been in the school of tears myself. Since then, I have stood by the bier of a father and mother and I have learned just a little and I need not any more shed the crocodile tear in seeking to comfort others.

Why is it that when trouble comes we always go to one who understands? Why do children go to Mother when in trouble? When a child wants a new toy, it goes to Father, but when trouble comes and it wants comfort, it goes to Mother. Do you know why? Mother knows better than Father what trouble is. Mother has shed more tears. Why do women pray better than men? Because they have known more trouble. Is there anyone in the world who can touch a sore or a cut as gently as Mother? Oh, man, oh, woman, thank God if you can look back to the picture of a kindly, Christian, sympathetic mother instead of one of these modern, painted, rouged, bob-haired butterflies, all fixed up for the Devil and dances and tea parties. God give us more old-fashioned mothers!

Many other reasons for tears might be given, but I shall mention but one or two more. I am thinking of the sinner's tears. How precious these tears are in His sight! I am thinking of the tears of Peter. You remember that night when the Christ, the Son of God and Son of Man, stood in the judgment hall. They beat Him, they mocked Him and scourged Him. Yet the pain in His heart, as Peter denied Him, was the greatest pain of all. But blessed be God, Peter could weep. And into the night he went and we read the blessed words, HE WEPT BIT- TERLY. But these bitter tears were sweet to Him. *For there is joy in the presence of the angels of God over one sinner that repenteth.*

The story is told of the angel who was sent to earth with orders to bring back the most precious thing he could find on earth. He flew down and searched from pole to pole. He delved into the bowels of the earth and explored the depths of the sea and the wonders of the air. He picked up a gold nugget, but as he looked upon it, he said, "No! No! This is not good enough for the King." He gathered a handful of the most precious diamonds, but halfway to heaven he stopped and blushed, and turned back to earth. He sought and sought, but nothing seemed precious enough. And then, while he stood musing in a glen, he heard a sob. He looked up and saw a sinner kneeling on a rock, and with drooping head, pouring out his heart to God for pardon and forgiveness. Even as he prayed, the tears started and fell down before the unseen angel. "Ah!" said the heavenly messenger, "I have found it," and holding a golden chalice under the rock, he caught one penitent tear and flew back in triumph to heaven and God, with the most precious thing on all the earth.

I am thinking of the tears of the lost in perdition — useless tears, hopeless tears, tears over lost opportunity. May God prevent that any of you should reject His mercy, but Now, Now, while it is called today, accept Him, and —

> Think of the tears this world has shed,
> Think of the tears the eyes made red,
> Think of the sorrows, trials, and care,
> Think of the Cross He had to bear.
>
> Think of the hearts that are broken by sin,
> Think of the souls He sought to win,
> But thwarted and gnarled in despair they lie
> Longing and wishing for a chance to die.
>
> Think of the moanings and groanings of life,
> Think of the woe and toil and the strife,
> Think of your faltering step by-and-by,
> Think of the tears in your then sightless eye.
>
> Think of the days when pleasure will fail
> At the end of the journey, as you set your sail

To realms over yonder, O what will it be:
More tears, or a blessed eternity?

'Twill either be weeping or gnashing of teeth,
Or wearing a crown and a bright laurel wreath.
'Twill either be God wipes all tears away,
Or forever to weep while the soul pines away.

Oh, what will it be when the call you shall hear
And the body's transferred from the bed to the bier?
Will your soul hear the shouting of heavenly joy,
Or be damned in the fires that will not destroy?

O what will it be, friend, tell me, I pray,
If the grim and dark angel should call you today.
Would it be tears, tears, tears, through eternity
Or all wiped away as His blest face you see?

I am thinking of the tears of Jesus — the tears He wept at the grave of Lazarus, the tears He wept over Jerusalem, the *strong crying and tears* which must have have fallen in Gethsemane for us. He wept that your eyes might be dried. He suffered that you might be saved. He is waiting now to dry away those tears if you will only let Him.

The last mention of tears in the Bible is this: *And God shall wipe away all tears from their eyes; and there shall be no more death, neither sorrow, nor crying, neither shall there be any more pain: for the former things are passed away* (Revelation 21:4). Happy day! There shall be No more crying. And one of God's handkerchiefs to dry those tears away will be the revelation to us of the FRUIT OF OUR TEARS. He will then reveal that our tears were not in vain. He will show us that all of them were recorded and every one remembered. He will open the veil and show that NOT ONE SINGLE THING which He sent upon us and over which we shed tears was without a purpose, but we shall then see what we know now by faith, namely, *that all things work together for good to them that love God.*

God says, *"Thou tellest my wanderings: put thou my tears into thy bottle: are they not in thy book?"* (Psalm 56:8). *For thou has delivered my soul from death, mine eyes from tears, and my feet from falling* (Psalm 116:8). *They that sow in tears shall reap in joy* (Psalm 126:5).

If we could push ajar the gates of life
And stand within and all God's workings see,
We could interpret all this doubt and strife
And for each mystery find the key.
But NOT TODAY; then be content, poor heart,
God's plans like lilies pure and white unfold;
We must not tear the close shut leaves apart,
Time will reveal their calyxes of gold.
And when after patient toil we reach the land
Where tired feet with sandals loosed may rest,
When we shall clearly know and understand,
I know that we shall say God's way was best.

CHAPTER 9

THE CHEMISTRY OF MAN

> And God said, Let us make man in our image, after our likeness; and let them have dominion over the fish of the sea, and over the fowl of the air, and over the cattle, and over all the earth, and over every creeping thing that creepeth upon the earth. So God created man in his own image, in the image of God created he him; male and female created he them (Genesis 1:26, 27).

A great many different and confusing ideas have been held by theologians throughout the ages as to just what constitutes the image of God. Some have said that man was created in the image of God in that he possessed intellect and the possibilities of spiritual knowledge, love and wisdom. They tell us that by sin the image of God was entirely lost in so far as man's holiness and ability to save himself was concerned. In another sense the image of God was not lost, but merely marred, so that, although man has lost his own free will and his ability to lift himself out of spiritual death, he nevertheless has retained his power to think and to love, his sense of justice and of right and wrong. None of the above, however, find any foundation in the Holy Scriptures.

The image of God in which man was created will be seen from a very careful study of the Word of God to consist in his "trinity and unity." As we all know, the Godhead consists in Three Persons: the Father, the Son and the Holy Spirit. These Three are but one God, yet eternally exist in Three Persons — Father, Son, and Holy Ghost — who are equal in all Their attributes of holiness, justice, eternity, infinity, truth and love. We read in Genesis 1 that God created man in His own image, that is, He created man also a trinity in unity consisting of a body, soul and a spirit. Yet man was but one person and consisted of these three distinct parts. That man did consist of these three parts is clearly taught in the record of creation. Genesis 2:7 declares *And the Lord God formed man of the dust of the ground* [BODY], *and breathed into his nostrils the breath of life* [SPIRIT]; *and man became a living soul* [SOUL]. The same is taught again in I Thessalonians 5:23: *And the very God of peace sanctify you wholly; and I pray God your whole* SPIRIT *and* SOUL *and* BODY *be preserved blameless unto the coming of our Lord Jesus Christ*. From the above passages it will be clearly seen that Adam, in his original creation, consisted of body, soul and spirit and that the redeemed Thessalonians to whom Paul was writing also consisted of body, soul and spirit.

This constitution of man is not generally accepted even among Christians. There are two schools, the one teaching that man is composed of body and soul only, and the other that he consists of body, soul and spirit. If no more were revealed in the Word of God than what we note from Genesis and Thessalonians, it would be sufficient to show that the latter is the correct view. Those who hold the body and soul theory, or, as it is technically called, "dichotomy," tell us that man has a soul and body like a beast, but that the soul has the faculties of God-consciousness and knowledge. The others who hold to "trichotomy," base the fact upon the clear teaching of Scripture and distinguish between man in God's image and the beasts which have no spiritual connection with their Creator.

It is necessary, however, to remember that the record given to us in Genesis 1:26 is the record of the unfallen creation of God. We find that Adam by his creation was allied to the three great realms comprehended in both Creator and creation. By his body Adam was allied with the earth. Chemically the body of the man differs not a particle from the earth out of which he was taken. The human body consists (like the body of animals) of about eighty-five per cent water (hydrogen and oxygen), calcium, sodium, iron, nitrogen, phosphorus, arsenic and a large number of other rarer elements. This allies him closely to the inorganic creation. By his soul Adam was allied to the other members of the race of intelligent creatures, at first his wife and later other men. By his spirit Adam was allied to God. It was through his spirit that he knew God, and loved God, and sought after God.

Three other distinctions which are characteristic of body, soul and spirit might be mentioned here. The body is the seat and the instrument of the senses. The body is the instrument of expression for the soul. The soul, on the other hand, is the seat of the emotions, of the feelings, of love, of sorrow and of sympathy. It was Mary who said, *My* SOUL *doth magnify the Lord, and my spirit hath rejoiced in God my Saviour.* Both soul and spirit were occupied in the matter of worship and fellowship with God. The spirit is the seat of the knowledge of God (I Corinthians 2:11). It is through the spirit that we have fellowship with God. It is through the spirit that we approach God, and when this spiritual channel becomes clogged, fellowship with God is rendered impossible.

This then is the constitution of man before the fall and again after being renewed by the Spirit of God. When Christ came into the world and became a human being, He took upon Himself a complete human nature. He had a body, a soul and a spirit, and thus can rightly be called the last Adam. We read in I Peter 2:24: *Who his own self bare our sins in this own* BODY *on the tree, that we, being dead to sins, should live unto righteousness: by whose stripes we were healed.* Again Christ said, *My* SOUL *is exceeding sorrowful, even unto death.* Finally, when He hung upon the Cross and His sufferings drew to a close, He said, *Father, into thy hands I commend my* SPIRIT. When Christ died His BODY was placed in the TOMB, His SOUL descended into HADES, and His SPIRIT was committed unto GOD. It will be clearly seen from the above that Christ had a body, a soul and a spirit.

This is the ideal dwelling place of God. God chooses to dwell in a house of three rooms. Before the fall He dwelt in Adam. In the case of the Tabernacle, we find that this same threefold consitiution was carried out. Adam was the temple of God and every subsequent temple is patterned after the original. Hence, the Tabernacle and the Temple presented a very striking similarity to God's temple, the redeemed man. It will be recalled that the Temple as well as the Tabernacle had an Outer Court in which stood the Altar of Burnt Offerings and the Laver of Cleansing. It was called the Court of the Gentiles and was the outermost compartment. It was the only one of the three compartments of the Tabernacle which was visible. In this Court of the Gentiles all the sacrifices were slain and hence it was the place of sacrifice.

The next compartment was the Holy Place in which stood the table of shew-bread, the golden candlestick and the Golden Incense Altar. It was in the Holy Place that the priests fellowshiped with each other. Here they ate the bread. Here they burned the incense, and here they communed one with the other and with God. It was the place of fellowship.

Then came the innermost compartment, the Holy of Holies, in which the Ark of the Covenant reposed. Hidden behind the veil dwelt the Lord Jehovah. Two never went into this place together. Once a year, all alone, the high priest went in for individual atonement, intercession and intimate communion. Alone with God he went to intercede for his people. It was the place of most intimate fellowship.

The Tabernacle, it will be seen, was patterned after the image of God. The Court of the Gentiles corresponds to the body. It is in the body where sacrifice is made. We are admonished in Romans 12:1 to present our bodies a living sacrifice, holy and acceptable unto God, which is our reasonable service. It was in the body that Christ bare our sins on the tree. The body is that which is visible to the world. It is the outermost part of our trinity.

Secondly, the Holy Place corresponds to the soul. The soul is the place of worship and of fellowship. As the priests came together in the Holy Place daily to partake of the shew-bread and to offer incense, so the purpose of the soul is to feed together with others upon God's bread of life and to exercise the fellowship of believers.

Thirdly, the spirit corresponds to the Holy of Holies, the place of intimate communion and fellowship with God alone. It is here where the real battles are waged, where the victory is gained, where God's power is brought down and where the secret prayer life of the Christian is accomplished. That the Temple of the Old Testament is a picture of the temple of the New Testament, namely, our bodies, is perfectly evident from the following passages of Scripture: I Corinthians 6:19: *What? know ye not that your body is the temple of the Holy Ghost which is in you, which ye have of God, and ye are not your own?* II Corinthians 6:16: *And what agreement hath the temple of God with idols? for ye are the temple of the living God; as God hath said, I will dwell in them, and walk in them; and I will be their God, and they shall be my people.*

When man fell, the image of God was not only marred but

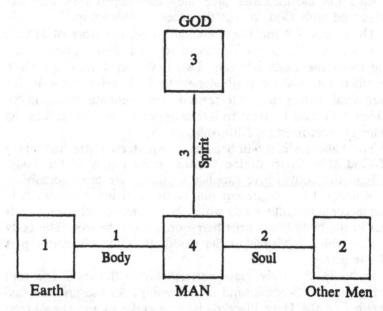

it was lost. Notice in the accompanying diagram how a man is related to the earth, to his fellow men and to God. Square No. 1 represents the earth. Square No. 2 represents our fellow man. Square No. 3 represents God. Square No. 4 represents man. The line No. 1 connecting square No. 1 stands for our body by which we are related to the earth. The line No. 2 connecting with square No. 2 signifies the soul through which we are in fellowship and relation to our fellow man. Line No. 3 connecting with square No. 4, represents the Spirit through which we have fellowship and union with God.

This is a diagrammatic picture of man in the image of God as he was created. God had said to Adam, *The day that thou eatest thereof thou shalt surely die.* Just what happened when Adam did eat of the forbidden tree? Certain it is that he did not die physically that day, for he lived over nine hundred years after that time. Equally clear it is that he did not die as far as his soul was concerned. He still had the ability to fellowship with his fellow creatures, to love, to sorrow, to rejoice and to mourn.

But the death was first of all a *spiritual* death. The moment Adam ate of the forbidden tree, he died spiritually. That is, his fellowship, his union with and his relationship to God were immediately broken. He broke with the Source of life and died. This is clearly evident from his conduct, for instead of seeking after God, he feared God, fled from Him and hid himself among the trees of the Garden. He was cut off from the Source of spiritual life. Line No. 3 was broken and although contact with the earth and other men continued for the term of physical life, man was out of touch with God. As a result he also died physically. This physical death began immediately, but did not culminate until nine hundred years after.

I may cut a flower with its stem from the plant. It is cut off from its source of life. It is potentially dead, but the actual withering process may be delayed by putting the stalk in water, which will keep it apparently alive for a few days. But the final result is death. So too, when man died spiritually, he was cut off from the Source of life and he continued to live physically for a time, but the result was bodily as well as spiritual death.

This, then, is the condition of man through sin. The image of God, which consists of body, soul and spirit, has been lost, and man now consists of a body and a soul, but he is spiritually dead. To this extent, then, man has become more like a brute beast than like God. A careful study of social conditions and moral conditions even among the most civilized people of the world will bear out this assertion. Since man lowered himself, as it were, to the level of a brute, God dealt with him in harmony with his degraded condition. Even his diet, which before the fall was limited to conform to his high position in the image of God, was changed so that it became more like the diet of a beast than that of a being made after the image of the Almighty.

A very interesting illustration of this fact is found in the first three chapters of Genesis. Man by his fall is out of touch with God. He does not seek after God but only lives for those things for which an animal lives. The two strongest and most deep-seated of all the instincts of man are self-preservation and self-propagation. The man outside of God, and outside of Christ, lives for these two things only. He may reach a high state of moral conduct, ethics, refinement and education, but every ambition of the unregenerate man, traced to its lowest, will be found to be selfish in the extreme. In this way man lowered himself in some instances apparently far below the unintelligent creation. This is seen very clearly in the curse which God pronounced upon man.

Notice first of all Genesis 1:11: *And God said, Let the earth bring forth grass, the herb yielding seed, and the fruit tree yielding fruit after his kind, whose seed is in itself, upon the earth: and it was so.* It will be seen from this verse that the earth at the word of the Lord brought forth two kinds of vegetation called "grass" and "herb yielding seed." The English translation is not clear. The Holland translation of this passage of Scripture is much closer to the original than the English. In the original language this passage indicates that God classifies herbs into two groups: those that bear edible seed, and those whose foliage, leaves, stalks, etc., are edible. In the Dutch the distinction is indicated by two words: the first is *grasscheutjes* and the second, *kruid zaad zaaiende*. The first word is translated in the English as "grass" and is used in the original to indicate all herbs and plants whose foliage is edible, such as lettuce, greens, onions, cress spinach, etc. The second class of herbs includes those whose fruit or fruit receptable is edible, such as beans, peas, tomatoes, egg plant, etc.

Turning to the twenty-ninth verse of the first chapter of Genesis, we notice that the former class of herbs called "grass" in Scripture was given for the food of beasts as well as the herb bearing seed. But man was limited in his vegetable diet to the herbs which *bore edible fruit.* (Genesis 1:29 and 30). *And God said, Behold, I have given you* EVERY HERB BEARING SEED, *which is upon the face of all the earth, and every tree, in the which is the fruit of a tree yielding seed; to you it shall be for meat. And to every beast of the earth, and to every fowl of the air, and to every thing that creepeth upon the earth, wherein there is life, I have given* EVERY GREEN HERB *for meat; and it was so.* The above two verses when read carefully will show this distinction.

This, however, was previous to the fall. When sin entered into the world through the disobedience of Adam and man broke with his God, he became spiritually dead and thereby lowered himself in his constitution to the level of the animals. And in perfect conformity with his fallen condition, God now supplied him with animal food. Genesis 3:17 and 18: *And unto Adam he said, Because thou hast hearkened unto the voice of thy wife, and hast eaten of the tree, of which I commanded thee, saying, Thou shalt not eat of it: cursed is the ground for thy sake; in sorrow shalt thou eat of it all the days of thy life; thorns also and thistles shalt it bring forth to thee;* and THOU SHALT EAT THE HERB OF THE FIELD.

In the last part of the eighteenth verse we read that part of the curse upon man for eating of the forbidden tree is the necessity of eating the herb of the field. Before the fall he was restricted in his diet to the "herb yielding seed." But now since sin has entered into the world, God adds to man's normal diet that class of herbs called "grass" in the Scripture. Here undoubtedly is the basic reason why children dislike that class of foods comprehended in the name of "grass." All parents who read these pages know how difficult it is to make our children eat those foods which are so necessary for their normal development, such as lettuce, spinach and cabbage. If they are anything like my children, grace alone will not perform the work, but law is needed. On the other hand, it is a well-known fact how fond children in general are of fruits. Does not this peculiarity of taste so generally found among the children under all circumstances go back to our original condition in Adam before the fall? Certain it is that this possibility is strongly suggested by the incident in the first three chapters of Genesis.

We have shown in the foregoing that man originally, as created by God, consisted of body, soul and spirit. By the fall, however, man's spirit died, and the natural man, unregenerated, consists of a living body and a distorted soul, but he is spiritually dead. If he has a spirit at all, it is a dead spirit. There is only one way in which an individual may again be restored to the image of God, and that is through a renewed contact with God by His Spirit. Man has concocted schemes without number in an effort to better himself and lift himself by the boot straps from his degraded position in sin to the higher life of God's image. Some have attempted to improve man by mortifying the body, or even sprinkling a little water upon it and calling it "baptism." Others have turned to education, training and legalizing the soul with equally unsatisfactory results. *Verily, verily, I say unto thee, Except a man be born again, he cannot see the kingdom of God.*

Man's trinity has been disrupted and can never be restored until the Spirit of God imparts within him a new nature. All attempts to fix up the body or soul must meet with failure. It is doing nothing more than a clever piece of undertaking work. The undertaker may patch up the body, putting on the paint and the rouge, smoothly patting down the hair, and dressing up the corpse so that it looks so lifelike and natural that one would almost expect it to sit up in the coffin, but it nevertheless remains a corpse and in a very short time will be as repulsive a corpse as if it had never been taken care of by the mortician.

In the same way Modernism today with its undertaker's tools of moral reform, ethical teaching, education and religion can only patch up the corpse. It takes a new creation to restore the spirit and bring man back into fellowship with God. No matter how moral, refined, educated, pious or dignified a man may be, if he has not been born again, he is a child of the

Devil, under the curse of God and destined to eternal separation from God. There is no truth that needs to be emphasized more in these last days than the truth that Christ expressed to the Pharisee Nicodemus when He said, *Verily, verily, I say unto thee, Except a man be born again, he cannot see the kingdom of God.*

Reader, have you been born again? By the sin of our first parents you have lost the image of the Creator. Adam, as the representative of the whole human race, caused the race to fall. As the oak tree is contained in the acorn, so was the whole human race contained in Adam our father. It is not a matter of arguing how justice could impute the sin of one to the whole race — but a matter of facing the fact. If a bear were caught in a steel trap, arguing about the injustice of the trapper in so placing the trap that he became ensnared would not liberate him. The first object must be how he may be made free, and then there will be plenty of time after being liberated to argue the justice of setting the trap. So too, all arguments which would refute the right of our Creator to include all of Adam's offspring in his sin are out of place. We are facing a fact. We know that the children suffer for the parents' sins. This is a matter of everyday observance and knowledge. The great question is: How may this condition be remedied? The same One whom men criticize because the whole race fell in Adam has also provided the remedy. As by one man sin entered into the world, so by the obedience of One, whosoever will may be saved. Adam sinned as a representative of the race. Jesus died as the Representative of a redeemed race. As Adam's sin was imputed to us without our works, so is the righteousness of Christ imputed to us without our works.

Will you accept Him? Will you receive Him? The moment you do, God gives you His Spirit and you become once more created in the image of God by faith in Jesus Christ. God grant that as this message goes forth many may be caused to turn to Him and live.